War seemed further away in early 1914 than it had done for many months. British warships sailed to ports in Germany on goodwill visits. The French President dined at the German Embassy, the first to do so for forty-four years. None of the national leaders wanted war; each knew a European conflict would be a holocaust of death and destruction. Yet war came.

Taking up the threads in 1870, this book examines the diplomatic, military and political origins of the war. The threads are followed through the maze of Bismarck's defensive treaties, through the gradual emergence of the fatal 'balance of power', through military developments which resulted in the 'nation in arms' in respective power blocs, through the successive upheavals in the Balkans, through the Anglo–German naval race, and on to the 1914 crisis and the bluffs, miscalculations and accidents which led to that holocaust which all had feared.

Over 150 extracts are given from contemporary documents. Speeches, private papers, official statements, diplomatic signals, war ultimatums—all are given to clarify and illustrate the tangled tragic origins of mankind's most hideous slaughter.

Illustrated throughout with pictures drawn from contemporary sources, this addition to the WAYLAND DOCUMENTARY HISTORY SERIES, offers an exciting and authentic approach to history studies.

Frontispiece German troops passing under the Arc de Triomphe in Paris during the Franco-Prussian War (1870)

The Origins of World War One

by Roger Parkinson

WAYLAND PUBLISHERS LONDON

Available in hardback (**limp edition also available*):

940.3
PAR

SBN (hardback edition): 85340 011 3
SBN (limp edition): 85340 211 6
Third impression 1973
Copyright © 1970 by Wayland (Publishers) Ltd
101 Grays Inn Road, London WC1
Photoset and printed by BAS Printers Limited, Wallop, Hampshire

Contents

The Illustrations

Preface

WAR came in summer 1914, yet no one wanted it. Least of all did the leaders of the Powers wish to start the holocaust which was to sweep Europe for four years and bring the deaths of thirteen million soldiers from fifteen different countries.

German industrialists, believing Germany would soon become the leading nation in Europe through economic and not military conquest, did not want war. Russia's leaders, troubled by nationalists, believed they would not be ready to fight a major continental war for another three years. In France, a general election had recently returned a pacific majority of Socialists and Radicals. In Britain, two-thirds of the Cabinet were against European involvement; and in the search for colonial possessions and markets, Britain now believed she could compete commercially with Germany. And Germany herself had become an excellent market for British goods.

In 1914 international tension seemed slightly lower than it had been in 1913. Poincaré dined at the German Embassy in Paris, the first French President to do so since 1870; British warships were on a goodwill visit to German ports even as the 1914 crisis was at its height; the race between Britain and Germany for bigger and better warships had been partially eclipsed by agreement on the Baghdad railway.

And yet war came. Why?

1 *The Future Participants*

GERMANY, the victor of the Franco–Prussian conflict of 1870, prospered under Bismarck. Exhilarated by military victory, confident, using the free trade within the empire, protected from the outside world by tariffs, German industrial wealth multiplied. The basic agrarian society was rapidly transformed.

But other transformations came more slowly. The German workers' movement became more important with industrialisation, and the Social Democratic Party (SPD) was formed in 1875. The manifesto or charter setting out its ideals was published in May. Known as the *Gotha Programme* it was basically a demand for a fair deal for the workers.

'Labour is the source of all wealth and of all civilisation; and since it is only through society that generally productive labour is possible, the whole product of labour, where there is a general obligation to work, belongs to society—that is, to all its members, by equal rights, and to each according to his reasonable needs. *The Gotha Programme*

'In the society of today the means of production are a monopoly of the capitalistic class; the dependence of the working class, which results from this, is the cause of misery and servitude in all its forms ...

'Proceeding from these principles, the socialist labour party of Germany endeavours by every lawful means to bring about a free State and a socialist society, to effect the destruction of the iron law of wages by doing away with the system of wage labour, to abolish exploitation of every kind, and to extinguish all social and political inequality ...

13

Facing page Leaders of Europe, *top left* (left to right) Kaiser Wilhelm II of Germany, Tsar Ferdinand of Bulgaria, Emperor Franz Joseph of Austria, Sultan Mehmed V of Turkey, *top right* the Kaiser speaking to the King of Italy, *bottom left* President Poincaré of France, *bottom right* Bethmann-Hollweg (caped) speaking to von Jagow (right)

'... the socialist labour party of Germany demands the following reforms in the present social organisation: (1) the greatest possible extension of political rights and freedom in the sense of the above-mentioned demands; (2) a single progressive income tax, both State and local, instead of all existing taxes, especially the indirect ones, which weigh heavily upon the people; (3) unlimited right of association; (4) a normal working day corresponding with the needs of society, and the prohibition of work on Sunday; (5) prohibition of child labour and all forms of labour by women which are dangerous to health and morality; (6) laws for the protection of the life and health of workmen, sanitary control of workmen's houses, inspection of mines, factories, workshops, and domestic industries by officials chosen by the workmen themselves, and an effective system of enforcement of the same; (7) regulation of prison labour (1).'

Yet the country was still firmly ruled by the Emperor and his Junkers class. The officer corps remained powerful, restricted and professional. Parliamentary franchise was limited and still favoured the country landlords despite the rapid growth of industrial populations. And though the Anti-Socialist Law, 21 October 1878, introduced by Bismarck, did not prohibit the candidature and election of socialists to the Reichstag, it tried to suppress everything that might help socialism spread:

Bismarck's Anti-Socialist Law (1878) 'Associations which aim, by social-democratic, socialistic or communistic agitation, at the destruction of the existing order in State or Society are forbidden ...

'Meetings in which social-democratic, socialistic, or communistic tendencies, directed to the destruction of the existing order in State or society, make their appearance are to be dissolved ...

'All printed matter, in which social-democratic, socialistic, or communistic tendencies appear ... is to be forbidden ...

'The collection of contributions for the furthering of social-democratic, socialistic, or communistic endeavours ... as also the public instigation to the furnishing of such contributions, are to be forbidden by the police ... (2)'

14   Nevertheless, the efforts of Bismarck and his successors could

Facing page A contemporary cartoon of 'the ablest statesman in Europe', Bismarck

not stop the steady Socialist pressures. Anti-Socialist legislation SPD
was not renewed in 1890, and a new SPD manifesto was adopted *Programme*
by the party in 1891.

It first stated the country's problems: '... Ever greater grows the
mass of the proletariat, ever vaster the army of the unemployed, ever
sharper the contrast between oppressors and oppressed, ever
fiercer that war of classes between bourgeoisie and proletariat,
which divides modern society into two hostile camps, and is the
common characteristic of every industrial country. The gulf
between the propertied classes and the destitute is widened by the
crisis arising from capitalist production, which becomes daily more
comprehensive and omnipotent, which makes universal uncertainty
the normal condition of society, and which furnishes a proof that
the forces of production have outgrown the existing social order,
and that private ownership of the means of production has become
incompatible with their full development and their proper application ...'

And then went on to the ways to solve them: '... the German
Social Democrats demand, to begin with:

'Universal, equal and direct suffrage by ballot, in all elections,
for all subjects of the Empire over twenty years of age, without
distinction of sex ...

'Direct legislation by the people by means of the right of initiative
and of veto ...

'Universal military education. Substitution of militia for a
standing army. Decision by the popular representatives of questions
of peace and war. Decision of all international disputes by arbi-
tration ... (3)'

Finally, in the November 1912 election there was a great Socialist
sweep to power.

The new politicians wanted a diminution of militarism and the
influence of the officer corps. In April 1913 the Army bill, with its
heavy tax burdens, was only approved after a bitter debate in the
Reichstag. The Krupp arms works were severely criticised. The
military class was even more disliked after the 'Zabern Affair' in
November 1913, when Lieutenant Baron von Forstner offered a

17

Facing page The famous *Punch* cartoon, 'dropping the pilot', at the time
of Bismarck's fall from power

reward of 10 marks to any of his soldiers who should succeed in running a dissident civilian through with his bayonet.

The position of Chancellor Bethmann Hollweg became increasingly precarious. Then in 1914 came an economic slump. If German militarism, the officer corps, and the Junkers class were to keep their positions, and if the heavy bills for the Army were to be paid in the future, it seemed it would have to be shown the Generals and the German Army were not merely eating the fat of the land.

Germany had already had an economic crisis in 1909, when a report prepared by Winston Churchill, President of the Board of Trade, was circulated to the Cabinet 3 November: '... The overflowing expenditure of the German Empire strains and threatens every dyke by which the social and political unity of Germany is maintained. The high customs duties have been largely rendered inelastic through commercial treaties, and cannot meet the demand. The heavy duties upon food-stuffs, from which the main proportion of the customs revenue is raised, have produced a deep cleavage between the agrarians and the industrialists, and the latter deem themselves quite uncompensated for the high price of food-stuffs by the most elaborate devices of protection for manufacturers. The splendid possession of the State railway is under pressure being continually degraded to a mere instrument of taxation. The field of direct taxation is already largely occupied by State and local systems. The prospective inroad by the universal suffrage Parliament of the Empire upon this depleted field unites the propertied classes, whether Imperialists or State-right men, in a common apprehension, with which the governing authorities are not unsympathetic. On the other hand, the new or increased taxation on every form of popular indulgence powerfully strengthens the parties of the Left, who are themselves the opponents of expenditure on armaments and much else besides ...'

The report continues that: 'These circumstances force the conclusion that a period of severe internal strain approaches in Germany. Will the tension be relieved by moderation or snapped by calculated violence? Will the policy of the German Government be to soothe the internal situation, or to find escape from it in external adventure? There can be no doubt that both courses are open ... But one of the two courses must be taken soon, and from that point of view it is of the greatest importance to gauge the spirit of the new administration from the outset. If it be pacific, it must soon become markedly pacific, and conversely (4).'

The Dual Monarchy of the Austro–Hungarian Empire was in constant danger of disintegration. The Austrians on the one side and the Hungarian Magyars on the other attempted to retain their power over the minorities in their respective parts. But these minorities—the Czechs, the Poles, the Ukrainians, the Serbs, the Italians—when totalled together outnumbered the ruling Austrian Germans and the Magyars.

Dissension increased especially after the 1905 Russian Revolution (cf below). But the biggest threat to the Empire came from the Slavs, some of whom were in the Austro–Hungarian area, and from others who were in the independent South Slav kingdom of Serbia. Others again were in the territory of Bosnia–Herzegovina, administered by Austria–Hungary after 1878. The Slavs themselves intrigued with Russia against the Hapsburgs.

Klofac, chairman of the National Socialists in Austria–Hungary, issued this memorandum in April 1914, after he had visited Russia to discuss Russian help for resistance: '... In eastern Moravia and in Silesia the secret aim of the secretariats should be the building up of a network based on every town and village so that in the case of a Russian advance across Silesia into eastern Moravia people should be available on whom the Russian army could completely rely ...'

But Shebeko, Russian Ambassador in Vienna, advised caution in a report to Sazonov, the Foreign Minister: '... Owing to the atmosphere of distrusts of everything Russian which is prevalent here, a feeling which is partly due to the careless behaviour of our agents, I think it necessary to ask my colleague Zhukovski (Russian consul in Prague) to be extremely careful in his contacts with local politicians and members of opposition parties, and to refrain from any action which might compromise our consular representation in Austria–Hungary ... (5)'

Dangers of agitation among Austro–Hungarian Slavs who wished to be joined with the independent Slavs increased after the murder of the Austrian-controlled King Milan of Serbia in 1903. Serbia then tried to throw off economic dependence on Austria; to do this she needed a good seaport, but Austria constantly attempted to stop Serbian efforts to acquire one. And Germany was tied to Austria, despite the dangers of involvement, because she was considered to be Germany's only reliable ally.

The 'Greater Turkey' Ideal

In Turkey, the dissolute Sultan Abdul Hamid II, responsible for the systematic massacre of the Christian Armenians in the 1890's, was opposed by the 'Young Turks' in 1908, many of whom had fled into Europe from his oppression. Despite his promise of a more liberal constitution, which he had made before in 1876, the Revolution was successful. But the rebels were later to practise barbarities as great as those of 'Abdul the Damned'. Moreover, they had visions of a 'Greater Turkey', extending wherever exiled Turks lived.

This nationalistic ideal was fully expressed in two works by Tekin Alp, *Thoughts on the Nature and Plan of a Greater Turkey*, and *The Turkish and Pan-Turkish Ideal*: 'There are now sixty to seventy million Turkish subjects of various states in the world ... Now that the Ottoman Turks have awakened from their sleep of centuries they do not only think of themselves but hasten to save the other parts of their race who are living in slavery and ignorance ... If all the Turks in the world were welded into one huge community, a strong nation would be formed ... (6)'

And again: 'The Pan-Turkish aspirations cannot come to their full ... realisation until the Muscovite monster is crushed ... If the Russian despotism is to be destroyed by the brave German, Austrian, and Turkish armies, thirty to forty million Turks will receive their independence. With the ten million Ottoman Turks this will form a nation ... advancing towards a great civilisation which may perhaps be compared to that of Germany ... In some ways it will be even superior to the degenerate French and English civilisations ... (7)'

20

Facing page Sultan Abdul Hamid II of Turkey

A Japanese cartoon of 1904 showing the spreading tentacles of the Russian octopus

In Russia, the declining rule of the autocratic Tzar was attacked by dissension within his vast, subjugated nation, and was eroded from without by the inept handling of the Russo–Japanese War, 1904–5.

Its disastrous effect on Russian prestige was described by Count Witte, Russian Finance Minister and made Prime Minister by the Tzar in 1905: 'Instead of enhancing the prestige and increasing the physical resources of the regime, the war, with its endless misery and disgrace, completely sapped the system's vitality and laid bare its utter rottenness before the eyes of Russia and of the world generally, so that the population, whose needs had been neglected for many years by a corrupt and inefficient government, finally lost patience and fell into a state of indescribable confusion (8).'

Witte on Russia

Revolution broke out in 1905. On 22 January, 'Bloody Sunday', one Father Gapon led an immense procession to present a peaceful petition setting out the grievances of the people, but affirming their loyalty to the Tzar: 'Sire: We workingmen and inhabitants of St.

Russian Workers' Petition (1905) 23

Facing page 'Bloody Sunday' in Russia (1905) showing Father Gapon's procession just before the troops opened fire

Petersburg ... come to Thee, Sire, to seek for truth and defence. We have become beggars; we have been oppressed; we are burdened by toil beyond our powers ... we are not recognised as human beings; we are treated as slaves ... We are choked by despotism and irresponsibility ... We have no more power, Sire; the limit of patience has been reached. There has arrived for us that tremendous moment when death is better than the continuation of intolerable tortures. We have left off working and we have declared to the masters that we shall not begin to work until they comply with our demands. We beg but little ...

Russian revolutionaries in 1905

'Sire, here are many thousands of us, and all are human beings only in appearance. In reality in us, as in all Russian people, there is not recognised any human right, not even the right of speaking, thinking, meeting, discussing our need ... We have been enslaved ...

24

under the auspices of Thy officials ...

'Sire, is it in accordance with divine law, by grace of which Thou reignest? ... We are seeking here the last salvation. Do not refuse assistance to Thy people ... Give their destiny into their own hands. Cast away from them the intolerable oppression of officials. Destroy the wall between Thyself and Thy people, and let them rule the country together with Thyself ... (9)'

However troops were assembled and ordered to shoot and over 1,500 marchers were slain. The repercussions spread wide. On 14 June sailors of the battleship *Potemkin* mutinied; in February, Grand Duke Sergius, Governor of Moscow, was killed. Russia was torn by riots, reprisals, and strikes, including the massive general strike in October.

The Government was helpless, and the Tzar, with Count Witte *'The October* as his newly appointed Premier, had to issue a manifesto on 30 *Manifesto'* October promising a bill of rights and a responsible Parliament.

This manifesto first deplored the unrest: 'The rioting and agitation in the capitals and in many localities of Our Empire fills Our heart with great and deep grief. The welfare of the Russian Emperor

Revolutionary barricades in Russia in 1905

25

is bound up with the welfare of the people, and its sorrows are His sorrows. The turbulence which has broken out may confound the people and threaten the integrity and unity of Our Empire.

'The great vow of service by the Tsar obligates Us to endeavour, with all Our strength, wisdom and power, to put an end as quickly as possible to the disturbance so dangerous to the Empire. In commanding the responsible authorities to take measures to stop disorders, lawlessness, and violence, and to protect peaceful citizens in the quiet performance of their duties, We have found it necessary to unite the activities of the Supreme Government, so as to ensure the successful carrying out of the general measures laid down by Us for the peaceful life of the State.'

Then it dealt with the new rights: 'We lay upon the Government the execution of Our unchangeable will:

'To grant to the population the inviolable right of free citizenship, based on the principles of freedom of person, conscience, speech, assembly and union.

'Without postponing the intended elections for the State Duma and in so far as possible, in view of the short time that remains before the assembling of that body, to include in the participation of the work of the Duma those classes of the population that have been until now entirely deprived of the right to vote, and to extend in the future, by the newly created legislative way, the principles of the general right of election.

'To establish as an unbreakable rule that no law shall go into force without its confirmation by the State Duma ... (10)'

The measures in this charter succeeded in splitting the liberals between the 'Octobrists', those who wished to accept the manifesto, and the extremists. They were thus an easier target. The authorities counter-attacked and the rebellion was stamped out. The Tzar issued decrees reversing the October manifesto, the first Parliament (Duma) was dissolved; but the seeds of revolution had been sown.

The Tzar and the Duma

The Tzar, helped by the split among the liberals and the raising of loans from foreign countries to help the economic situation, recovered his position. The first Duma was dissolved with the following Proclamation on 21 July 1906, the second suffered

26

a similar fate, while the third supported the Government. 'We summoned the representatives of the nation by Our will to the work of productive legislation. Confiding firmly in divine clemency and believing in the great and brilliant future of Our people, We confidently anticipated benefits for the country from their labours. We proposed great reforms in all departments of the national life. We have always devoted Our greatest care to the removal of the ignorance of the people by the light of instruction, and to the removal of their burdens by improving the conditions of agricultural work.'

The Tzar tries to justify his action: 'A cruel disappointment has befallen Our expectations. The representatives of the nation, instead of applying themselves to the work of productive legislation, have strayed into spheres beyond their competence ... In short, the representatives of the nation have undertaken really illegal acts, such as the appeal by the Duma to the nation.

'The peasants, disturbed by such anomalies, and seeing no hope of the amelioration of their lot, have resorted in a number of districts to open pillage, and the destruction of other people's property, and to disobedience of the law and of the legal authorities. But Our subjects ought to remember that an improvement in the lot of the people is only possible under conditions of perfect order and tranquillity ...

'In dissolving the Duma We confirm Our immutable intention of maintaining this institution, and in conformity with this intention We fix March 5, 1907, as the date of the convocation of a new Duma ... With unshakeable faith in divine clemency and in the good sense of the Russian people, We shall expect from the new Duma the the realisation of Our efforts and their promotion of legislation in accordance with the requirements of a regenerated Russia (11)'

The French defeat by the Prussians in 1871 resulted in the pro- *France* clamation of a republic by the people of Paris and the formation of the Government of National Defence. But the republicans, associated with the campaign to continue the war, were defeated in the 1871 elections—yet the new Assembly, with a large royalist majority, was only allowed to last two months before being thrown out by a revolution in Paris.

Open rebellion broke out on 18 March 1871, and the Paris Commune took over power, issuing a manifesto on 19 March: 'By its revolution of the 18th March, and the spontaneous and courageous efforts of the National Guard, Paris has regained its autonomy ... On the eve of the sanguinary and disastrous defeat suffered by France as the punishment it has to undergo for the seventy years of the Empire, and the monarchial, clerical, parliamentary, legal and conciliatory reaction, our country again rises, revives, begins a new life, and retakes the tradition of the Communes of old and of the French Revolution. This tradition, which gave victory to France, and earned the respect and sympathy of past generations, will bring independence, wealth, peaceful glory and brotherly love among nations in the future. Never was there so solemn an hour ... (12)'

From then on, despite the anti-republican forces, the democratic forces were strong enough to control the military aristocracy. A number of serious clashes did, however, still take place, notably the Dreyfus Affair which began in 1894. Captain Alfred Dreyfus, a Jew, was accused of military espionage, and although it later appeared he was obviously innocent, the military authorities refused, until 1906, to accept the fact. They objected to the interference in military affairs. The Dreyfus controversy, which included the publication of Zola's famous letter in the newspaper *L'Aurore* in 1898, played an important part in the 1902 elections, when the republican forces won a large majority. But although the military class was kept under tight civilian control, France was still a 'nation in arms'. And the desire in France to regain the territories of Alsace and Lorraine, taken by Germany after the Franco–Prussian war, remained strong.

Zola's important letter *'J'accuse!'* was published on 13 January 1898; it is clear from this final section how it got its name: '... I accuse Generals de Boisdeffre and Gonse of having made themselves accomplices in the same crime—the one, no doubt, led on by clerical passion, the other perhaps by that "esprit de corps" which makes of the War Office Bureax an ark holy and not to be touched.

Facing page Emile Zola, who strongly protested at the handling of the Dreyfus affair

'I accuse General de Pellieux and Commandant Ravary of having turned their inquiry into a work of villainy, by which I mean that the inquiry was conducted with the most monstrous partiality; and that of this partiality the report of Ravary is an imperishable monument, brazen in its audacity …

'I accuse the War Office of having carried on in the press … an abominable campaign intended to lead astray opinion and hide its

Captain Alfred Dreyfus sketched during his trial

misdoings.

'Lastly, I accuse the first court-martial of having violated right by condemning an accused man on a document which was kept secret, and I accuse the second court-martial of having shielded this illegality to order, committing in its turn the judicial crime of acquitting a man they knew to be guilty (13).'

Britain, protected by the Channel and her powerful fleets, managed to stay isolated from European entanglements. Her army was small, professional, and involved in colonial peace-keeping.

One of the clearest, and most famous, declarations of the principles of British foreign policy at the turn of the century was given by Sir Eyre Crowe, Senior Clerk at the Foreign Office, 1906–12: 'The general character of England's foreign policy is determined by the immutable conditions of her geographical situation on the ocean flank of Europe as an island State with vast overseas colonies and dependencies, whose existence and survival as an independent community are inseparably bound up with the possession of preponderant sea power.

Eyre Crowe on British Foreign Policy

'Sea power is more potent than land power, because it is as pervading as the element in which it moves and has its being. Its formidable character makes itself felt the more directly that a maritime State is, in the literal sense of the word, the neighbour of every country accessible by sea.'

So, he continues:

'It would, therefore, be but natural that the power of a State supreme at sea should inspire universal jealousy and fear, and be ever exposed to the danger of being overthrown by a general combination of the world.

'The danger can in practice only be averted—and history shows that it has so been averted—on condition that the national policy of the insular and naval State is so directed as to harmonise with the general desires and ideals common to all mankind, and more particularly that it is closely identified with the primary and vital interests of a majority, or as many as possible, of the other nations.

'Now, the first interest of all countries is the preservation of national independence.

'It follows that England, more than any other non-insular Power, has a direct and positive interest in the maintenance of the independence of nations, and therefore must be the natural enemy of any country threatening the independence of others, and the natural protector of the weaker communities.'

To achieve this, power must be equal:

'The equilibrium established by such a grouping of forces is technically known as the balance of power, and it has become almost an historical truism to identify England's secular policy with the maintenance of this balance by throwing her weight now in this scale and now in that, but ever on the side opposed to political dictatorship of the strongest single State or group at a given time.

'If this view of British policy is correct, the opposition into which England must inevitably be driven to any country aspiring to such a dictatorship assumes almost the form of a law of nature (14).'

When she did reluctantly become more involved in central European affairs, Britain's traditional relationships were closer to Germany than France. But inside the British Isles a liberalism which echoed the French republicans gathered strength, until in the 1906 elections the Liberals came into the House of Commons with an overwhelming majority of 356. Lord Salisbury, Prime Minister and Foreign Secretary since 1885, had retired in 1902. With him had gone his friendly attitude towards Germany and his cool detachment from Continental entanglements. His successor, Balfour, resigned in 1905. The Conservative Party, discredited by the handling of the Boer War, alienated from the workers by the Taff Vale decision, further weakened by the tariff protection issue, was pushed aside. The way was open for dramatic domestic liberal reforms. But the Irish question, simmering since Gladstone had begun his campaign in 1886 to give Ireland home rule, was linked with the struggle between the Liberal House of Commons and the Conservative House of Lords, and attention was further distracted from foreign affairs.

On 12 July 1912, Bonar Law, the new Tory leader, stated: 'There are things stronger than parliamentary majorities. I can imagine no length of resistance to which Ulster people will go in

Facing page The Marquis of Salisbury whose sympathies had been pro-German

which I shall not be ready to support them.'

By 1914, the Irish situation had deteriorated further. Churchill was to write later: 'The preparations of the Ulstermen continued. They declared their intention of setting up a provisional Government. They continued to develop and train their forces. They imported arms unlawfully and even by violence ... Volunteers were enrolled by thousands, and efforts were made to procure arms. As all this peril grew, the small military posts in the North of Ireland, particularly those containing stores of arms, became a source of preoccupation to the War Office (15).'

Inside the British Army itself, there were strong unionist sympathies. According to Asquith the Prime Minister: 'His information from the War Office with regard to the attitude of the Army was of a serious character, pointing to the probability of very numerous resignations of commissions of officers in the event of the troops being used to put down an Ulster insurrection. Some of the authorities estimated the number of these resignations as high as thirty per cent. He did not believe in this figure, but he was satisfied that there would be a number of resignations (16).'

Indeed, on 20 March 1914, the extent of this support within the Army was reflected in the Curragh 'mutiny', when, after being asked if they would undertake active operations against Ulster, the brigadier in the area and fifty-seven out of seventy officers said they would rather be dismissed.

Churchill as So German diplomats were naturally confident in 1914 that
First Lord the British were so occupied and divided by these domestic issues, with the Irish struggle approaching widespread civil war, that they would not intervene in a distant Balkan conflict. However, as Winston Churchill, who had been made First Lord of the Admiralty in 1911, said in the Commons on 28 April 1914: '... I will venture to ask the House once more at this moment in our differences and quarrels to consider whither it is we may find ourselves going ... Apart from the dangers which this controversy and this Debate clearly show exist at home, look at the consequences abroad.

34   'Anxiety is caused in every friendly country by the belief that

To test against air attack, a naval plane flies over one of the harbour forts
at Spithead in England (1912)

for the time being Great Britain cannot act. The high mission of
this country is thought to be in abeyance, and the balance of
Europe appears in many quarters for the time being to be deranged.
Of course, foreign countries never really understand us in these
islands. They do not know what we know, that at a touch of external
difficulties or menace all these fierce internal controversies would
disappear for the time being, and we should be brought into line
and into tune. But why is it that men are so constituted that they
can only lay aside their own domestic quarrels under the impulse of
what I will call a higher principle of hatred? (17)'

2 Europe: The Diplomatic Chequer Board 1871–1913

THE 1871 PEACE terms were harsh. Not only was money exacted by the Germans from the French, but also territory—Alsace and most of Lorraine. The conquered provinces remained as a constant irritant to both Germany and France. Because as Bismarck himself declared: 'Not one voice in France has renounced Alsace–   *Bismarck* Lorraine; at any moment a government may be established which will declare war ... (when it came) ... on both sides an effort will be made to finish the adversary, to bleed him white, that the vanquished may not be able to rise again, and may never for thirty years dare even to think of the possibility of turning conqueror(18).'

Bismarck, suspicious of the French, feared a renewal of the anti-Prussian coalition of the time of Frederick the Great—Austria, France and Russia. So the German Chancellor began his diplomatic manipulations to protect his country through secret treaties. In October 1873 a close agreement between Austria, Russia and Germany was concluded.

But in 1875 came a war scare when rebellion broke out in the Turkish-ruled province of Bosnia-Herzegovina. Austria–Hungary feared a collapse of Turkish power would allow Serbia to secure an outlet to the Adriatic, and agreement was reached with Russia for Austrian control over the area should the Turks be forced out. Instead, the Turks recovered, and the Russians, still feeling the need for a warm water seaport, took the opportunity to begin war with Turkey in 1877.

The conflict ended with the Peace of San Stefano, resulting in a large Bulgaria with a frontage on the Aegean. But this alarmed

37

Facing page top the war in Herzegovina (1875), a Turkish post near Kostanitza, *below* Austrian troops occupying Bosnia after the Treaty of Berlin (1877)

Austria, and also Britain, and a British fleet was sent to the Dardanelles. Under this pressure the Tzar submitted his San Stefano Treaty to revision. Bulgaria was sliced into three parts. Bosnia and Herzegovina came under Austrian control, but remained nominally under Turkish sovereignty, with far-reaching consequences. The complicated arrangement was put like this in the Treaty of Berlin:

Article 25 read: 'The provinces of Bosnia and Herzegovina shall be occupied and administered by Austria–Hungary. Since the Austro–Hungarian Government does not desire to undertake the administration of the Sanjak of Novibazar, which extends between Serbia and Montenegro in south-east direction to beyond Mitrovitsa, the Ottoman administration will continue to function. Nevertheless in order to assure the maintenance of the new political state as well as the freedom and safety of communications, Austria–Hungary reserves the right to maintain garrisons and to have military and trading roads over the whole area of that portion of the ancient Vilayet of Bosnia. To this end the Governments of Austria–Hungary and Turkey propose to come to an agreement over the details (19).'

However, this increase in Austro–Hungarian power caused concern, and the Italians were among those apprehensive over the arrangement. The Italian Prime Minister, Cairoli, telegraphed to Corti, the Ambassador at Constantinople on 30 June 1878: 'It goes without saying that the Austrian occupation of Bosnia in our eyes is and ought to be provisional.' But it wasn't and the continued occupation became another source of disagreement between Rome and Vienna. Crispi, the Italian Minister for Home Affairs, told the Chamber in March 1880: '... By the Treaty of Berlin, Austria acquired with Bosnia and Herzegovina an invulnerable frontier in the Near East and ought to rest content. We without envying her ill-gotten gains must be willing that she shall stay there, but that she shall not ask for more than the treaty gives her. We, gentlemen, in our own interests and in accordance with the principles of our great revolution must be the protector and friend of the little states in the Near East ... (20)'

All the arrangements were ratified in 1878 by the Congress of

Disraeli speaking with Bismarck during the Congress of Berlin (1878)

Berlin. Disraeli returned to England saying: 'I bring you Peace with Honour'. But while the Berlin Treaty may have settled the near-Eastern crisis, it did not settle the Near-Eastern question.

Moreover, the treaty angered the Russians, and Bismarck feared a closer union between France and Russia as a result. To protect Germany, he proposed an alliance with Austria, and a secret treaty was concluded directed against the possibilities of a Russian attack: *Austro-German Alliance (1879)*

The Austro–German Alliance, 7 October 1879: 'Should, contrary to the hope and the sincere desire of the two high contracting parties, one of the two Empires be attacked by Russia, the high contracting parties bind themselves to come to the assistance of each other with the whole military strength of their Empire and accordingly only to conclude peace in common and by mutual agreement.

39

'Should one of the high contracting parties be attacked by another power, the other party binds itself hereby not only to refrain from assisting the aggressor against its high ally, but to observe at least a benevolent neutral attitude towards its fellow contracting party.

'Should, however, the attacking party in such a case be supported by Russia, either by active co-operation or by military measures which constitute a menace to the party attacked, the obligation of reciprocal assistance with the whole fighting force which is stipulated in Article 1 of this treaty becomes equally operative, and the conduct of the war by the two high contracting parties shall in this case also be joint until the conclusion of a common peace ...

'This treaty shall, in conformity with its peaceful character, and to avoid any misinterpretation, be kept secret ... (21)'

But the Tzar himself was in difficulties. The war against Turkey had increased revolutionary opposition to the ruling class. Alexander II was assassinated, and his successor Tzar Alexander III realised even more the need for support. And so on 18 June 1881, Russia, Germany and Austria signed a secret treaty, the League of the Three Emperors.

League of the Three Emperors (1881)

The agreement was to strengthen the countries' relations: 'The Courts ... of Austria–Hungary, of Germany, and of Russia, animated by an equal desire to consolidate the general peace by an understanding intended to assure the defensive position of their respective States, have come into agreement on certain questions which more especially concern their reciprocal interests.

'In case one of the high contracting parties should find itself at war with a fourth Great Power, the two others shall maintain towards it a benevolent neutrality and shall devote their efforts to the localisation of the conflict ...

'Russia, in agreement with Germany, declares her firm resolution to respect the interests arising from the new position assured to Austria–Hungary by the Treaty of Berlin.

'The Three Courts, desirous of avoiding all discord between them, engage to take account of their respective interests in the Balkan Peninsula ... (22)'

41

Facing page The Tsar in the uniform of a Cossack. *Overleaf* The League of the Three Emperors triumphantly celebrated in Berlin

Triple Alliance
(1882)

Negotiations were also successful for the inclusion of Italy into the Austro–German alliance, with Italy motivated by fears of French colonial activities in Africa. The result was the Triple Alliance Treaty, of 20 May 1882 signed by Italy, Germany and Austria.

According to the terms of the Alliance: 'The high contracting parties mutually promise peace and friendship, and will enter into no alliance or engagement directed against any one of their States. They engage to proceed to an exchange of ideas on political and economic questions of a general nature which may arise, and they further promise one another mutual support within the limits of their own interests ...

'If one, or two, of the high contracting parties, without direct provocation on their part, should chance to be attacked and to be engaged in a war with two or more Great Powers nonsignatory to the present treaty, the "casus foederis" will arise simultaneously for all the high contracting parties.

'In case a Great Power nonsignatory to the present Treaty should threaten the security of the States of one of the high contracting parties, and the threatened party should find itself forced on that account to make war against it, the two others bind themselves to observe towards their Ally a benevolent neutrality. Each of them reserves to itself, in this case, the right to take part in the war, if it should see fit, to make common cause with its Ally.

'If the peace of any of the high contracting parties should chance to be threatened under the circumstances foreseen by the preceding articles, the high contracting parties shall take counsel together in ample time as to the military measures to be taken with a view to eventual co-operation. They engage henceforward, in all cases of common participation in a war, to conclude neither armistice, nor peace, nor treaty, except by common agreement among themselves.

'The high contracting parties mutually promise secrecy as to the contents and existence of the present treaty (23).'

The Alliance was renewed in 1887, 1891, 1902 and 1912. But even this treaty system was not enough to reassure Germany. It had to be backed by a powerful German army.

Revolution in Roumelia (1885) showing Serbian troops on the march

And not only France had to be checked, but also Germany's semi-ally, Russia. In 1885 a revolt in Bulgaria reopened the Balkan question, and once again there was the possibility of a Russian thrust south. So in June 1887 the so-called 'Reinsurance Treaty' was concluded by Germany and Russia, supplementing, from the German viewpoint, the agreements with Austria–Hungary.

Reinsurance Treaty (1887)

It's terms declared: 'In case one of the high contracting parties should find itself at war with a third great Power, the other would maintain a benevolent neutrality towards it, and would devote its efforts to the localisation of the conflict. This provision would not apply to a war against Austria or France in case this war should result from an attack directed against one of these two latter Powers by one of the high contracting parties.

'Germany recognises the rights historically acquired by Russia in the Balkan Peninsula, and particularly the legitimacy of her preponderant and decisive influence in Bulgaria and in Eastern

Roumelia. The two Courts engage to admit no modification of the territorial status quo of the said peninsula without a previous agreement between them, and to oppose, as occasion arises, every attempt to disturb this status quo or to modify it without their consent ... (24)'

Bismarck in the Reichstag

But simmering continued in the Balkans and the threat from France remained. On 6 February 1888, Bismarck told the Reichstag: '... God has given us on our flank the French, who are the most warlike and turbulent nation that exists, and He has permitted the development in Russia of warlike propensities which until lately did not manifest themselves to the same extent ... (25)'

Bismarck's Resignation Letter (1890)

By now it appeared that treaties were insufficient. Military force seemed a better guarantee of safety. Bismarck was seen by fellow-Germans as over-subtle. And with the admission that treaties were indeed not enough, Bismarck himself was finished. He was forced to resign on 18 March 1890, and his policies were altered, including the Chancellor's policy of friendly relations with

Bismarck on Britain

Britain summed up in a speech he made in the Reichstag on 26 January 1889, describing Britain as 'the old traditional ally with whom we have no conflicting interests.'

In his letter of resignation, Bismarck puts the blame on the attitude and policies of the Kaiser: '... It is very painful to me, in my attachment to the service of the Royal House, and to Your Majesty, and after long years of familiarity with conditions which I had regarded as permanent, to sever myself from the accustomed relations with Your Majesty and the general policy of the Empire and of Prussia; but after conscientious consideration of Your Majesty's intentions, which I should have to be prepared to carry out were I to remain in the service, I cannot do otherwise than most humbly beseech Your Majesty graciously to please to release me, with the statutory pension, from the offices of Imperial Chancellor, Prime Minister, and Prussian Minister of Foreign Affairs.

'After my impressions of the last few weeks and the disclosures which I gathered yesterday from the communications of Your Majesty's Civil and Military Cabinets, I may in all respects assume that I am meeting Your Majesty's wishes by this my request for leave to resign, and I may also with safety assume that Your Majesty will graciously grant my request.

'I would have submitted the request for my discharge from my office to Your Majesty a long time ago, if I had not had the impression that it was Your Majesty's wish to make use of the experience and the capacities of a faithful servant of your predecessors. Now that I am sure that Your Majesty does not require these, I am able to retire from public life, without the fear that my decision will be condemned as untimely by public opinion (26).'

With Bismarck gone, a choice was made between closer union with Russia or Austria, rather than the delicate manoeuvrings with both which the Chancellor had attempted, and the Germans decided on Austria. A sinister influence was exercised on German foreign relations by Holstein, who, hating Bismarck, was determined to change his policies. In addition, the mental health of the young Kaiser Wilhelm II began to cause increasing concern.

Bismarck told von Poschinger in 1892: 'In the last few months before my dismissal the question constantly occupied my mind in sleepless nights whether I could endure things any longer under him. Love for my country told me "You must not go, you are the only one who can still serve as a counterpoise to his will." But on the other hand I knew the Monarch's mental state which opened up in my mind prospects of the most lamentable complications. The drama in Bavaria connected with King Ludwig II which ran its course relatively smoothly would, in a military state like Prussia, have assumed a more disastrous and difficult character. Then the Kaiser himself put an end to my inward struggle by intimating that he no longer wanted me (27).'

Bismarck on his Dismissal

In Russia, the need for security sufficiently overcame the Tzar's fear and dislike of republicanism for him to form the Franco–Russian Convention of 1892–3, designed to give protection against Germany for the duration of the Triple Alliance. In 1899 the Treaty was amended so that it would continue even if the Triple Alliance should collapse.

Franco-Russian Military Convention (1892)

According to the terms of the Convention: 'France and Russia,

47

being animated by an equal desire to preserve peace, and having no other object than to meet the necessities of a defensive war, provoked by an attack of the forces of the Triple Alliance against one or another of them, have agreed upon the following provisions:

'If France is attacked by Germany, or by Italy supported by

President Kruger of South Africa

Germany, Russia shall employ all her available forces to attack Germany.

'If Russia is attacked by Germany, or by Austria supported by Germany, France shall employ all her available forces to fight Germany.

'In case the forces of the Triple Alliance, or of one of the Powers composing it, should mobilise, France and Russia, at the first news of the event and without the necessity of any previous concert, shall mobilise immediately and simultaneously the whole of their forces and shall move them as close as possible to their frontiers (28).'

These terms were to provide an excuse and justification for mobilisation.

Britain reluctantly ended Salisbury's isolationist policy and entered the search for allies, one reason being the German support for the Boers against Britain, including the sending of a telegram from the Kaiser to Kruger on 3 January 1896. The telegram read: 'I sincerely congratulate you that, without appealing for the help of friendly Powers, you with your people, by your own energy against the armed hordes which as disturbers of the peace broke into your country, have succeeded in re-establishing peace and maintaining the independence of your country against attacks from without (29).'

Kruger Telegram (1896)

In 1898 an approach for an alliance was made to Russia by Britain but was rejected. There was still the traditional feeling of hostility between Britain and France. Joseph Chamberlain, British Colonial Secretary, therefore turned to the only major power left in Europe—Germany. The Germans themselves, wanting Britain in the Triple Alliance system, had long sought some agreement with Britain providing it was on German terms.

Moltke and England

According to Moltke: 'Among the Great Powers, England necessarily requires a strong ally on the Continent. She would not find one which corresponds better to all her interests than a United Germany, that can never make claim to the command of the sea (30).'

The Germans therefore tried to strike a hard bargain. Yet the Kaiser visited Windsor in the early days of the Boer War, and platitudinous speeches were uttered. One had an unexpected result. On 30 November after the Kaiser had left England, Chamberlain made the following speech at Leicester on the lines agreed between him and Bülow. Instead of helping Anglo–German relations, it did the reverse, with indignation breaking out in each

Chamberlain's Anglo-German Speech

49

country at the thought of dealing with the other: '... We have had our differences with Germany, we have had our quarrels and contentions: we have had our misunderstandings. I do not conceal that the people of this country have been irritated and justly irritated

Prince Bernhard von Bülow

by circumstances which we are only too glad to forget, but at the root of things there has always been a force which has necessarily brought us together. What then unites nations? Interest and Sentiment. What interest have we which is contrary to the interest of Germany?

'I cannot conceive any point which can arise in the immediate future which would bring ourselves and the Germans into antagonism of interests. On the contrary I can see many things in the future which must be a cause of anxiety to the statesmen of Europe, but in which our interests are clearly the same as the interests of Germany ... (31)'

Chamberlain caricatured by *Punch*

But Germany's Foreign Minister Bülow believed the longer he waited the more would be obtained. He told Kaiser Wilhelm II in 1900: 'Your Majesty is quite right in feeling that it is the English who must make the advances to us. They have just had quite a drubbing in Africa, America proves to be uncertain, Japan unreliable, France full of hatred, Russia perfidious, public opinion in all countries

Bülow on Anglo-German Relations

51

hostile ... now it gradually dawns on the English that they can no longer maintain their world empire solely by their own efforts against so many adversaries ... In view of the general world situation and of our own vital interests, Your Majesty would accomplish a real master stroke, if without Your Majesty's prematurely binding Yourself or making explicit declarations Your Majesty could produce the impression in responsible English circles that there was hope of a future solidly-based relationship with us. The threat of an English agreement with the Dual Alliance is only a threatening apparition to scare us, which the English have been using for years ... (32)'

Chamberlain   However, Britain's Chamberlain tried to avoid a treaty which was too precise.

This attempt to avoid details which could lead to a strict commitment is shown in the following passage from Chamberlain's Leicester speech: '... I have used the world "alliance" ... but again I desire to make it clear that to me it seems to matter little whether you have an alliance which is committed to paper, or whether you have an understanding in the minds of the statesmen of the respective countries. An understanding is perhaps better than alliance which may be a stereotype arrangement which cannot be regarded as permanent in view of the changing circumstances from day to day ...'

Negotiations faltered and finally failed. In Britain, the Kruger telegram had not been forgotten. In Germany, Bülow delivered an anti-British speech to the Reichstag in December 1899, and Britain turned to Japan instead.

Chamberlain   The attempt to bring about Anglo–German agreement had
writes   obviously failed completely by the end of the year; Chamberlain
Germany Off   wrote the following sentences to Baron von Eckardstein, Secretary at the German Embassy in London, on 28 December: 'I will say no more here about the way in which Bülow has treated me. But in any case I think we must drop all further negotiations on the question of the Alliance ... Everything was going on well, and even Lord Salisbury had become quite favourable, and in entire agreement with us, as to the future developments of Anglo–German

Facing page King Edward VII of England

relations. But alas it was not to be.'

Later, Chamberlain was to say: 'So long as Bülow is in power, I will not move another finger for an understanding with Germany (33).'

Anglo-French Overtures
As a means of restraining Russia's advance in the Far East, an Anglo–Japanese Alliance was signed in January 1902. Russia in turn moved closer to France with a joint statement that they would consult together on means for safeguarding interests in the Far East. Britain was alarmed by the possibility of Russo–French co-operation, and at last turned to Paris in the hope of agreement.

To the astonishment of both sides, progress was remarkably smooth, despite traditional hostilities. By April 1904 several Franco–British agreements had been signed, and the Anglo–French 'Entente Cordiale' had been created, to the relief of Britain and to renewed fears of encirclement in Germany. This was shown when Paul Cambon, French Ambassador in London, told King Edward VII in 1904: 'The true cause of the nervousness which seems to have afflicted Wilhelm for several months is that he never would believe in the possibility of an Anglo–French accord; he continued to speculate on the misunderstanding between our two countries as he did on all the germs of discord that exist between the Powers; he had sought to get himself regarded as supreme arbiter of Europe, the defender and guarantor of the general peace; in a word, he expected to play the leading role everywhere. And he sees with bitterness Your Majesty taking this role from him (34).'

German Anxiety
The dismay of the German government is shown, when on 31 May 1906, Bülow wrote to the Kaiser expressing his fears over the Entente: 'We must therefore not allow Vienna to perceive either that we have too great a need of support from Austria or that we feel ourselves in any way isolated. The Austrians must have the impression that in any event we have full confidence in ourselves. Therefore we must represent our relations with Russia, Italy, and England as better than they actually are and even refrain from showing, for example, our resentment against Italy (35).'

This is in marked contrast to 1900 (p. 51) when the Germans were confident of their diplomatic position and strength. A Military Bridge

Holstein, now the main influence on German foreign policy, said the Entente should be smashed by force if necessary. The Kaiser apparently agreed: on 1 May 1904, when opening a new bridge over the Main, he said that if the bridge were to be 'used for more important traffic, it would perfectly fulfil its purpose (36).'

But Bülow, elevated to the Chancellorship in 1900, decided instead to interfere in the sensitive area of North Africa. He began secretly to support the Sultan of Morocco against the French, who had in effect been given the territory by the British under the terms of the Entente. In addition, Bülow advised the Kaiser to visit Tangier, and he reluctantly agreed. *German Gauntlet*

Bülow told him: 'Through your Majesty I threw down the gauntlet in challenge to the French to see whether they would mobilise (37).'

This move was little more than an excuse to try and make war.

The French refused to aggravate the conflict over Morocco by mobilising troops. But they did agree to the German demand for a Moroccan Conference, which opened at Algeciras in January, 1906. Britain's new Liberal Foreign Minister, Sir Edward Grey, gave full support to the French. Only Austria stood by Germany. It was a diplomatic defeat for Germany, and Holstein was forced to resign.

The Anglo–French Entente had been tested and found successful; *Closer Entente* the French, more confident now, were determined to stand up to the Germans in the future. Britain felt the same. And as Sir Edward Grey, the British Foreign Secretary, wrote afterwards: 'The wind of armed German pressure, though it had swept M. Delacassé out of the Foreign Office in 1905, had in the long run only caused France to draw the cloak of the "Entente" with Britain more closely about her (38).'

Moreover, France refused to sympathise with the republican *Russia and the* opposition to the Russian Tzar, despite French pretensions to be *Entente* the home of Liberty, and gave him full financial support in the 1905 Revolution. Britain also looked to Russia and the Anglo–Russian Entente was signed in August 1907. Moves to bring about closer

55

union had started after the conclusion of the agreement with France.

Edward VII, while visiting Denmark soon after the conclusion of the Anglo–French agreement had told the Russian Ambassador in Copenhagen: '... Since by mutual goodwill a solution has been found to the disputes which had dragged on for years between England and France, this gives me the hope of arriving by the same method at still more important results, ie a similar agreement with Russia ... My new Ambassador, Sir Charles Hardinge, is to have instructions to work for the establishment of the most cordial relations with the Russian Government and to seek means of reaching agreement on the questions dividing us at the different points of the globe (39).'

Indeed, as with the Anglo–French Entente, Britain and Russia found the need for an ally could overcome mutual suspicions.

And so the Triple Alliance was balanced by the Triple Entente. Germany was surrounded. Traditional fears were realised. But this 'balance of power' was itself flimsy. And in the years between 1907 and 1914 a succession of events occurred which showed this shakiness. The 'spheres of influence' were ragged and in dispute.

Germany, increasingly isolated after the Algeciras Conference, was forced to rely more on Austrian support. This meant Berlin had to follow Vienna's initiatives.

At the end of 1907 Austria proposed to annex Bosnia–Herzegovina, already administered by her since 1878. Annexation would, it was hoped, cut the ties between the south Slavs in the area and Serbia, that 'revolutionary nest'. Germany, in the person of Schoen, who had become Foreign Secretary in 1907, had to promise support with reluctance and with claims by the Kaiser that he had not been kept informed.

Serbian Time Bomb

Indeed, Aehrenthal, Austro–Hungarian Foreign Minister, had to calm down original statements from Vienna with this communication to the German Chancellor on 8 December, so making it easier for the Germans to give their cautious support: 'Our policy is guided by the wish not to create conflict with Serbia. We shall persevere in this attitude also in the immediate future and believe

57

that, by so doing, we serve the general need for peace. However, we do not intend to prolong indefinitely this policy of patience. If in the course of the next two months the behaviour of Serbia gives us fresh reasons for serious complaint, then the moment will come at which we shall take a definite decision. In this eventuality I intend, in order to obviate a further extension of the conflict, to declare forthwith to the other Powers that we are carrying out only an act of natural self-defence (40).'

The Serbs, however, regarded Bosnia as the centre of national feeling.

In 1870 Kallay, Austro–Hungarian Finance Minister, had written: 'It (Bosnia) is the sensitive spot of all political minded Serbs, the centre round which revolve their aspirations and their hopes.'

Ninčić, Serbian Foreign Minister, wrote: 'There was a feeling that irreparable harm had been done, that we were on the eve of national disaster, and that Austria–Hungary, the implacable enemy of Serbia and the Serb race, was preparing to destroy every symptom of resistance in a people who wanted to live independent (41).'

As a result of the annexation the Serbs appealed to Russia, Serbian and Austrian troops faced one another. War seemed likely at any moment.

But Russia, weakened by the conflict with Japan and the 1905 Revolution, was in no state for war. Britain was unwilling to become involved. And the Tzar capitulated. In the first real test between the Triple Entente and the Triple Alliance, the latter had won. It was also a dress rehearsal for the 1914 crisis.

Russia vowed it must never happen again. A large arms pro-gramme was immediately started. France, after her treatment in 1905, had already begun a complete military reorganisation, and the two countries were drawn closer together. Serbia was also further embittered; nor was the Slav problem solved.

Asquith Fears   Asquith, who had only recently become the British Prime
On European   Minister, described the British attitude towards the events in the
Peace   Near-East in an important speech on 9 November: '... I do not

wish it to be supposed that we desire to see Europe divided into two

Three Russian battleships sunk during the 1905 Revolution

separate groups in connection with the new situation in the Near East. We have found ourselves in complete sympathy with France, who is the ally of Russia; but at the same time we, and I believe other Powers also, have been equally frank in our communications with Germany and Italy, who are the allies of Austria; because we recognise that the common object of Europe ought to be to overcome the difficulties which have already arisen without creating new difficulties, and that this can only be done by a policy which springs from general consent. Diplomatic victories may be too dearly bought. One Power's success may be so achieved as to involve another's disappointment and discomfiture; and thereby the very kind of friction is engendered which it should be the aim of a wise diplomacy to avoid ... Our sole objects are these: to maintain the public law of Europe; to secure for the new regime in Turkey just treatment and a fair chance; and to promote such an adjustment of the varied interests and susceptibilities which are

59

involved as will prevent a disturbance of the peace and open a road to freedom and good government ...'

Trying to calm things down he continued:

'A variety of circumstances has recently caused the relations between Great Britain and Germany to become a subject of active public discussion. It is almost exactly a year since the German Emperor was the guest of your predecessor, in this very hall. Some of us, and I was one, who were present on that occasion, cannot forget his Majesty's emphatic and impressive declaration that the governing purpose of his policy was the preservation of the peace of Europe and the maintenance of good relations between our two countries. It is in the spirit of that declaration, the spirit which aims not only at peace but at goodwill, that we desire to deal with other nations, with Germany not less than others ... May I submit to you and to others outside and beyond these walls, that there should be no talk at such a time of isolation, of hostile groupings, of rival combinations, among the Powers; those Powers who are the joint trustees of civilisation, and of its greatest and paramount safe-guard—the peace of the world! (42)'

The Triple Alliance also suffered from the crisis. Italy had shown herself to be a doubtful partner, with inclinations to negotiate separately with Russia, both countries hoping to gain the other's consent for Near East territorial ambitions. Britain tried to im-prove relations with Germany, but Germany felt acutely isolated, with the knowledge Italy was unreliable and with the belief Austria, like Germany itself, would act only in her own interests—and would perhaps act even more violently in the future.

German Military Hysteria Apprehension about Austria was, for example, caused by pas-sages in an article in *Danzer's Armee-Zeitung*, closely connected with the Austro–Hungarian Chief of Staff, which appeared on 7 January, 1909:

'Never was a war more just. And never yet was our confidence in a victorious issue more firmly grounded.

'We are being driven into war: Russia drives us, Italy drives us, Serbia and Montenegro drive us, and Turkey drives us ...

'We have formally taken possession of Bosnia which has long

been ours. Under the stress of circumstances we shall now lay hand on Serbia and, by our protection, give that sorely-tried land the chance of beginning a new life under our protectorate and of growing mature for the Pan-Serb idea—for a Greater Serbia under the Hapsburg sceptre. Montenegro, after the necessary rectification of our frontiers, we shall give back to Turkey, if the Porte remains neutral. Montenegro can then enjoy in full measure the blessings of a free rejuvenated Turkey.

'Full of the zest of battle the army awaits the tasks to which it is called.

'We go into battle with the consciousness that on us depends the future of our Empire. If we return victorious, we shall not only have conquered a foreign land: we shall have won back Austrian self-respect, given new life to the Imperial idea and vanquished not only the foreign enemy but the enemy in our midst.

'Our blood throbs in our veins, we strain at the leash.

'Sire! Give us the signal! (43)'

According to Bethmann Hollweg, successor to Bülow: 'In the year of 1909, the situation was based on the fact that England had firmly taken its stand on the side of France and Russia in pursuit of its traditional policy of opposing whatever Continental Power for the time being was the strongest; and that Germany held fast to its naval programme, had given a definite direction to its Eastern policy, and had moreover to guard against a French antagonism that had in no wise been mitigated by its policy in later years. And if Germany saw a formidable aggravation of all the aggressive tendencies of Franco–Russian policy in England's pronounced friendship with this Dual Alliance, England on its side had grown to see a menace in the strengthening of the German Fleet and a violation of its ancient rights in our Eastern policy. Words had already passed on both sides. The atmosphere was chilly and clouded with distrust (44).'

Bethmann Hollweg: 'Atmosphere Chilly'

This feeling was strengthened by the Second Morocco crisis of 1911. A Franco–German Treaty of 1909 had been aimed at settling the dispute over the interests of the two countries in Morocco, but by 1911 the treaty was clearly unworkable. Each suspected the other of trying to extend control. A Franco–German consortium for the development of the Congo also collapsed.

Lloyd George:
'War if . . .'

French troops were sent to Fez on 21 May 1911. In reply, a German warship, the *Panther*, arrived in Agadir harbour on 1 July. Britain reacted strongly, with a stern warning given by Lloyd George, then Chancellor of the Exchequer, to the Bankers' Association in a speech at the Manison House on 21 July:

'I believe it is essential in the highest interests not merely of this country, but of the world, that Britain should at all hazards maintain her place and her prestige amongst the Great Powers of the world. Her potent influence has many a time been in the past, and may yet be in the future, invaluable to the cause of human liberty. It has more than once in the past redeemed continental nations, who are sometimes too apt to forget that service, from overwhelming disaster and even from national extinction. I would make great sacrifices to preserve peace. I conceive that nothing would justify a disturbance of international goodwill except questions of the gravest national moment. But if a situation were to be forced upon us in which peace could only be preserved by the surrender of the great and beneficent position Britain has won by centuries of heroism and achievement, by allowing Britain to be treated where her interests were vitally affected as if she were of no account in the Cabinet of nations, then I say emphatically that peace at that price would be a humiliation intolerable for a great country like ours to endure ... (45)'

German
Destiny

This time it was the Triple Entente that emerged the winners in the clash with the Triple Alliance. Italy and Austria gave only weak support to Germany. The Germans, humiliated, accepted a settlement with the French which consisted mainly of useless French Congo territory.

In Germany encouragement was given to the naval programme and the fierce resentment against Britain was expressed when Heydebrand, the German Deputy, stormed in the Reichstag on 9 November: 'Now we know where our enemy stands. Like a flash of lightning in the night, these events have shown the German people where its enemy is. The German people now knows when it seeks its place in the sun, when it seeks the place allotted to it by destiny, where the State is which thinks that it can decide this matter ... When the hour of decision comes we are prepared for sacrifices, both of blood and of treasure (46).'

France, however, had been drawn nearer to Britain, and at the same time attempted to clarify the British position if France and Germany were to be at war.

On 28 March 1912 the French Prime Minister telegraphed the French Ambassador in London: 'The essential thing is that England shall not undertake to remain neutral between France and Germany even in the hypothesis of the attack seeming to come from our act (47).' *Burden of the Entente*

And Russia, while advising Paris to be cautious, had qualified this advice with the statement by the Tzar: 'You know our preparations are not complete.'

In September 1911, Italy broke still further away from Germany. The recognition of the French protectorate in Morocco had made Italy fear the French might next select Tripoli as a colonial target. In addition, with the disintegration of European Turkey likely, Austria stood a chance of gaining Near-Eastern territory at the expense of Rome. Italy therefore decided to strike first. Delivering an obviously unacceptable ultimatum to Turkey, she attacked Tripoli. The situation in the Balkans flared into conflict between the Balkan States and Turkey, with Italy attempting to gain control of the coveted Tripoli. At the end of 1912 the Turks were rapidly defeated and almost driven from Europe, a sign that the centuries long domination of the Balkans by Turkey was drawing to a close.

Austria and Italy immediately drew together again. Austria was determined Serbia should not retain an Adriatic seaport, which she stood a good chance of doing with the disintegration of the Turkish Empire, while Italy, with Turkey weakened, was determined to have the Albanian coastline to herself. Russia and Austria mobilised against each other. Again, Germany was forced to give at least nominal support to her Austrian ally.

And yet none of the Powers wanted war. Negotiations took place in early 1912 between Britain and Germany which continued into

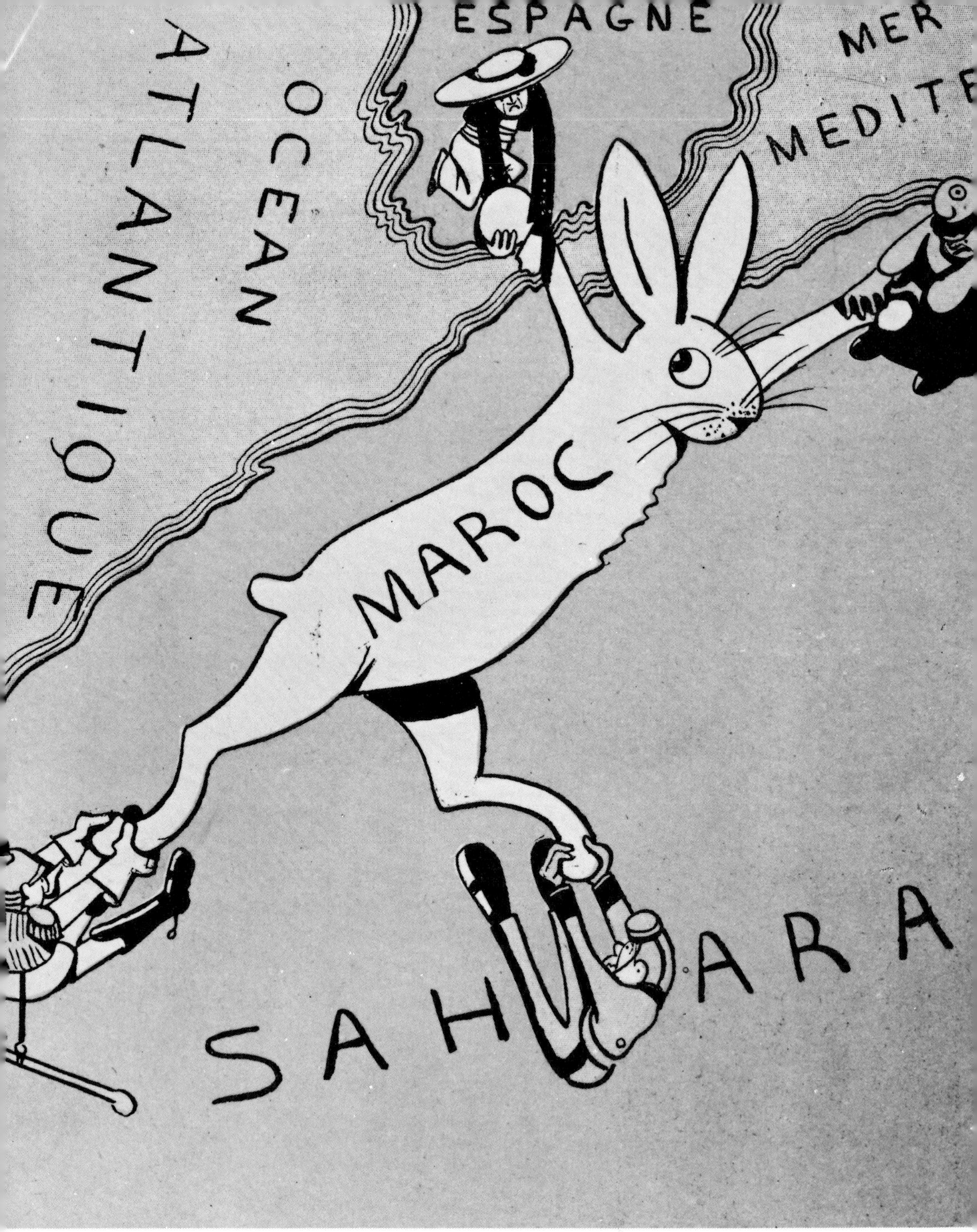
ESPAGNE
MER
MEDITE
OCEAN
ATLANTIQUE
MAROC
SAH ARA

the period of the Balkan crisis. Lord Haldane, Secretary of State for War, visited Berlin in March, but a formula for agreement put forward by the German Chancellor was rejected as one-sided.

These were the main points: 'The high contracting parties assure each other mutually of their desire of peace and friendship.

'They will not either of them make or prepare to make any (un-provoked) attack upon the other, or to join in any combination or design against the other for purpose of aggression, or become party to any plan or naval or military enterprise alone or in combination with any other Power directed to such an end, and declare not to be bound by any such engagement.' *German Peace Formula*

In case of conflict:

'If either of the high contracting parties becomes entangled in a war with one or more Powers in which it cannot be said to be the aggressor, the other party will at least observe towards the Power so entangled a benevolent neutrality, and will use its utmost endeavour for the localisation of the conflict. If either of the high contracting parties is forced to go to war by obvious provocation from a third party, they bind themselves to enter into an exchange of views concerning their attitude in such a conflict.'

However:

'The duty of neutrality which arises out of the preceding article has no application in so far as it may not be reconcilable with existing agreements which the high contracting parties have already made.

'The making of new agreements which render it impossible for either of the parties to observe neutrality towards the other beyond what is provided by the preceding limitation is excluded in conformity with the provisions in article 2 (48).'

Britain later gave these reasons for her rejection of the German formula: 'These conditions, although in appearance fair as between the parties, would have been grossly unfair and one-sided in their operation. Owing to the general position of the European Powers, and the treaty engagements by which they were bound, the result of articles 4 and 5 would have been that, while Germany in the case of a European conflict would have remained *Rejected by Britain*

65

Facing page The struggle for Morocco, a famous contemporary French cartoon

free to support her friends, this country would have been forbidden to raise a finger in defence of hers (49).'

Britain made her own proposals, only to be rejected by the Kaiser, who wanted an absolute pledge of British neutrality.

British Peace Formula The formula put forward by the British Cabinet in 1912 would have required a reciprocal agreement by Germany: 'The two Powers being naturally desirous of securing peace and friendship between them, England declares that she will neither make nor join in any unprovoked attack upon Germany. Aggression upon Germany is not the subject and forms no part of any treaty understanding or combination to which England is now a party, nor will she become a party to anything that has such an object (50).'

The Kaiser and Serbia Nevertheless, the desire on the part of the Powers for peace did make possible the long discussions on the Near East which started in London in December 1912. The seven-month conference was a success, despite the stumbling block of the question of a Serbian seaport, until the Austrians, fearing a Serbian *fait accompli*, sent Serbia a seven-day ultimatum in October 1913. The Kaiser gave his support, telling Conrad, Chief of the Austro–Hungarian General Staff, in an interview at Leipzig on 18 October: '... You may count upon my support. The others are not ready and will make no effort to prevent your action. You must be in Belgrade in a couple of days ... (51).'

But the Austrian ultimatum to Serbia, on the grounds that Serbian troops were positioned over the border in Albania, was more for diplomatic than military purposes.

According to the Austrians:

'It is indispensable in the eyes of the Imperial and Royal Government that the Serbia Government shall proceed to the immediate recall of the troops who have advanced beyond the frontiers fixed by the London meeting and who consequently occupy territories forming part of Albania. The Imperial and Royal Government is pleased to hope that the Serbian Government will not delay in proceeding the total evacuation of Albanian territory within a period of one week. Failing this, the Imperial and Royal Government will to its great regret find itself compelled to have recourse to the appropriate means to assure the fulfilment of its demand (52).'

Russia, for the third time, advised the Serbs to wait. And the result of this, the third major clash between the Triple Alliance bloc and the Triple Entente powers, was an Austro–German triumph. The Serbs, heeding the Austrian's threat of war, gave way, giving their reasons as follows: 'Animated now as ever by a pacific policy, very conscious of the seriousness of the situation in the Balkans and in the interests of the peace of Southern Europe, the Royal Government, desirous on the other hand of afresh giving the proof of its deference towards the Great Powers and of its friendship both towards them and towards the new Albania, has this very day issued the order to its troops to retire on the frontiers fixed by London, in spite of their not yet having been definitely fixed on the spot (53).' *Serbians Give Way*

The withdrawal left the impression that threats and ultimatums were more certain of success than diplomatic conferences. And the question of Serbia still remained. Russia was now more than ever committed to support that small country in the future. As the Tzar said: 'For Serbia we shall do everything.' On the other hand, Austria too was still unsatisfied. The situation was ready for the fatal and final crisis of 1914.

3 1870–1914 The Mechanics of Total War

OF ALL military theorists, Karl von Clausewitz is one of the most quoted. Unfortunately he is also one of the most misquoted, ever since his famous *On War* was first published in the 1830's.

This Prussian officer has been held to be the advocate of mass, total warfare, of the supreme importance of moving superior forces to crush the enemy completely in large-scale battle, and of the need for politicians to stand aside when war began and leave the running of the country to the generals. Plenty of quotations could be found in *On War* to support these alleged beliefs: 'War therefore is an act of violence intended to compel our opponent to fulfil our will ... Superiority in numbers is the most important factor in the result of a combat ... The destruction of the enemy's military force is to be sought for principally by great battles ... the chief object of great battles must be the destruction of the enemy's main force ... Let us not hear of Generals who conquer without bloodshed.' And of all quotations from Clausewitz, the most famous words attributed to him are: 'War is a continuation of politics by other means.' This was taken to mean that when war began, war should take over from politics, the generals from the politicians.

The followers of Clausewitz controlled the armies of Europe in the nineteenth and early years of this century. And they were guilty of oversimplifying Clausewitz to the point of gross distortion. Battles were indeed important, he said, but he added they may not actually have to happen. The threat of battle could be sufficient to gain victory: 'Possible combats are on account of their results to be looked upon as real ones ... The decision by arms is for

69

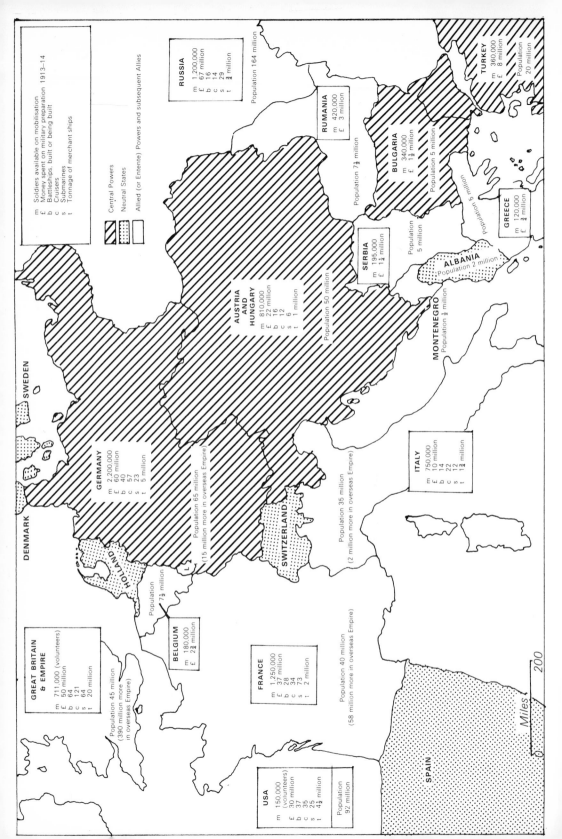

Legend:

m Soldiers available on mobilisation
£ Money spent on military preparation 1913–14
b Battleships, built or being built
c Cruisers
s Submarines
t Tonnage of merchant ships

Central Powers

Neutral States

Allied (or Entente) Powers and subsequent Allies

RUSSIA

m	1,200,000
£	67 million
b	16
c	14
s	29
t	⅓ million

Population 164 million

TURKEY

m	360,000
£	8 million

Population 20 million

RUMANIA

m	420,000
£	3 million

Population 7½ million

BULGARIA

m	340,000
£	1½ million

Population 5 million

SERBIA

m	195,000
£	1¼ million

Population 5 million

GREECE

m	120,000
£	¾ million

Population 5 million

ALBANIA
Population 2 million

MONTENEGRO
Population ½ million

AUSTRIA AND HUNGARY

m	810,000
£	22 million
b	16
c	12
s	6
t	1 million

Population 50 million

GERMANY

m	2,200,000
£	60 million
b	40
c	57
s	23
t	5 million

Population 65 million
(15 million more in overseas Empire)

ITALY

m	750,000
£	10 million
b	14
c	22
s	14
t	1½ million

Population 35 million
(2 million more in overseas Empire)

SWITZERLAND

HOLLAND
Population 7½ million

DENMARK

SWEDEN

GREAT BRITAIN & EMPIRE

m	711,000 (volunteers)
£	50 million
b	64
c	121
s	64
t	20 million

Population 45 million
(390 million more in overseas Empire)

BELGIUM

m	180,000
£	2¾ million

FRANCE

m	1,250,000
£	37 million
b	28
c	34
s	73
t	2 million

Population 40 million
(58 million more in overseas Empire)

USA

m	150,000 (volunteers)
£	30 million
b	37
c	35
s	25
t	4½ million

Population 92 million

SPAIN

Miles 200

all generations in war, great and small, what cash settlement is in trade.'

In other words, there need not be actual cash settlement (battle); more trade, or barter could be undertaken as a form of payment. Nor was the destruction of the enemy always necessary or even desirable: 'There are many ways to one's object in War; the complete subjugation of the enemy is not essential in every case.' If the enemy could be put into a position where he knew it was useless to continue, then peace should be sought by the victor without further bloodshed.

Above all, Clausewitz did not advocate the generals taking over from politicians. Indeed, he warned against it. The words attributed to him: 'War is a continuation of politics by other means'—were misconstrued. The essence of his thought is contained in this sentence: 'War is not only a political act but also a real political instrument, a continuation of political commerce, a carrying out of the same by other means.' (Book I, Chapter I, Section 24). By this he meant not that war is *the* instrument of politics and a country's leaders have no other choice but to use it. He meant that war is just one of the instruments open to political leaders, and if chosen, should be subject to the same political controls as any other method of conducting a nation's business. War, he believed, was not an independent thing in itself. If it was allowed to be, with generals in total control, there would be war for the sake of war, and 'we have before us a senseless thing without object'. Instead, war should only be fought for a clearly defined political purpose: 'The political object, as the original motive of the war, will be the standard for determining both the aim of the military force and also the amount of effort to be made.' War, therefore, should be tailored to the political aim; if the aim is limited, then the conduct of the war should be limited.

An analysis of Clausewitz is important because it shows where the handling of World War One went wrong. Because he was misinterpreted, war was fought by the generals with insufficient political control. It fed upon itself. Attempts were made to gain limited political objectives with massive, unlimited, military methods.

71

Facing page The strength of the Powers in 1914

The elder Moltke said: 'The politician should fall silent the moment mobilisation begins.' Clemenceau made the retort: 'War is too serious a matter to be left to the generals.' But he himself showed his preoccupation with fighting and lack of attention to the search for possible peace; in his speech to the French Chamber in 1917 he declared: 'You ask me for my policy. It is to wage war. Home policy? I wage war. Foreign policy? I wage war. All the time, in every sphere, I wage war.'

Indivisibly linked with the misinterpretation of Clausewitz was the development of the means of conducting mass war. The industrial revolution gave mass production; weapons could be made in sufficient numbers to supply mass armies; conscription was elaborated to supply the manpower.

A Nation in Arms   Railways increased mobility. Before, military movements had been dictated by the need to live off the country or from limited supply wagons or stocks. Now, supplies could come quickly from rear areas. This meant in turn that the whole nation was involved in the war, in providing supplies for the conflict. The nation became the nation in arms.

The most descriptive exposition of this total involvement of a nation in war had been given, in front of its time, by France many years before. It was now copied and developed far beyond anything the French could have hoped for: 'The young men shall fight; the married men shall forge weapons and transport supplies; the women will make tents and clothes and will serve in the hospitals; the children will make up old linen into lint; the old men will have themselves carried in to the public squares and rouse the courage of the fighting men, to preach hatred against kings and the unity of the Republic.

'The public buildings shall be turned into barracks, the public squares into munition factories ... All firearms of suitable calibre shall be turned over to the troops: the interior shall be policed with shot-guns and cold steel (54).'

At the same time, railways, while giving greater mobility, resulted in less flexibility. Armies were tied to railway tracks. Operational plans looked like railway timetables. And they also robbed the

The Gatling gun, the first really successful machine gun

battlefield of its ability to bring final victory. Because of the railway re-supply system, and the new telegraph communications, damage could be repaired and the gaps plugged. Yet because of the increased firepower of the new weapons, this damage became progressively greater.

The first successful machine gun was designed in America by Richard Gatling in 1862. Its drawback was the need to have a hand crank, but Sir Hiram Maxim's gun, invented in 1885, did away with this handle by using recoil energy. The British Army adopted this gun in 1889 and a larger Maxim was used in the Boer War, firing 37 mm shells called 'pom-poms'.

Invention followed invention throughout the century. In 1841 Prussia adopted the Dreyse needle-gun, the first practical breech-loading—as opposed to muzzleloading—rifle in Europe. Following

73

its success in the 1866 'Seven Weeks' War', every army in Europe began to use some form of breechloading rifle: the Hagstorm in Sweden, the Carte in Prussia, the Carcano in Italy, the Chassepot in France. During the century, British soldiers had a succession of different and improving rifles: the Baker, Minie, Enfield, Snider, Martini-Henry, Lee-Metford and Lee-Enfield.

Improved military explosives came at the same time—TNT, tetryl, picric acid, PETN and cyclonite. High explosive artillery shells came into use in the 1870's. Artillery itself improved in four main aspects: rifling, breechloading, interior ballistics and better recoil mechanisms.

In 1870 it seemed the Prussians demonstrated how all the improvements up to that date could be brought together in the most successful way possible. The apparently devastating defeat of the French by the Prussians under the elder Moltke's leadership seemed the copy-book pattern to follow, comprising the application of Clausewitz's alleged theories, rapid movement of mass striking force, emphasis on the offensive, and tight professional control by Staff Officers. Victory inflated the Germans with confidence. As

German Military Confidence (1871)

Sir Robert Morier, in the victorious Prussian capital, wrote on 27 January 1871: 'Such unparalleled successes as those which have attended the German arms, and the consequent absolute power which the German nation has acquired over Europe, will tend especially to modify the German character, and that not necessarily for the better. Arrogance and overbearingness are the qualities likely to be developed in a Teutonic race under such conditions, not boasting or vaingloriousness. I was painfully struck in my visit to the camp at Metz in October by the extraordinary difference I witnessed in this respect between the language and *tenue* of the officers I met there and those I had observed in the days which preceded the invasion of France. Is it love of exaggeration to fear that under such circumstances the German Empire based on universal suffrage, ie on the suffrages of the 800,000 men who have been fighting in France ... may have some of the faults of militarism attaching to it? (55)'

Other nations believed if they copied the German methods, rapid victory was certain. Essential qualifications and conditions mentioned by Clausewitz were overlooked or deliberately forgotten, including the emphasis he placed on the necessary relationship between political and military authority, with the former the most important; some passages containing this emphasis were cut from German editions of *On War*.

Yet to believe the increased firepower brought by improved weapons gave added strength to the offence, as opposed to the defence, meant overlooking the fact that this defensive firepower had made it extremely difficult to cross the last 400 yards of the battlefield.

Moltke himself insisted that frontal attacks were difficult, if not disastrous in view of modern firepower. The decisive battle must come through encirclement, the basic tactic he had tried to adopt in 1870: '... Little success can be expected from a mere frontal attack, but very likely a great deal of loss. We must therefore turn towards the flanks of the enemy's position ... (56)'

Moltke's Military Theory

However, as firepower continued to become ever more devastating, some theorists did begin to doubt the ability of the offensive to overcome the defence by means of a direct charge. They believed troops would either have to disperse, or encircle, in order to attack.

Soon after the Franco–Prussian war a German tactical manual stated 'the frightful effects of our fire-arms necessitate dispersion', and Captain Boguslawski, in his *Tactical Deductions from the War of 1870–71*, agreed: '... Great clouds of skirmishers and small tactical units, that is the form for infantry ... All idea of attacking with large compact masses, or of drawing them up in line to fire upon one another, is finally exploded ... (57).'

But this dispersion lessened the chances of tight control over the troops. And as early as the 1880's the shift began back towards a rigid firing line advancing to the attack. To overcome the greater firepower, more and more men would be thrown into the offensive.

A German Field Exercise in 1888 states: '... Every engagement intended to be of a decisive character will entail the occupation of the entire space available for deployment by a dense fighting line ...'

advancing head erect, and this was stressed still further in the 1895 regulations (58).

Lessons provided by the Boer War and the Russo–Japanese War were either ignored or soon forgotten. In France, the emphasis on the offensive as laid down by Foch, author of *The Principles of War* (1903) and fated to be supreme commander of the allied armies in France for the closing stages of the 1914–18 war, dominated tactics.

Foch, in his *Principles*, made full use of Clausewitz, as he misinterpreted him. He quotes the Prussian author: 'Blood is the price of victory. You must either resort to it or give up waging war.' He also quotes Von der Goltz, whose *Nation in Arms* (1883) had attempted to link the meaning of Clausewitz with the nation in arms concept: 'Modern wars have become the nation's way of doing business.'

French Military Theory The French soldier-theorist, armed with the authority of these two writers, goes on to say: 'Of all faults, only one is degrading, namely inaction.' Foch therefore believed battle should constantly be sought, using maximum numbers of troops, and the enemy 'torn to pieces'.

In his book on war he expresses his ideas more fully:

In chapter 3: '... modern war knows but one argument: the tactical fact, battle. In view of this it asks of strategy that it should both bring up all available forces together, and engage in battle all these forces by means of tactical impulsion in order to produce the shock.'

And in chapter 10: '... In order to reach its end—which is the imposing of our will on the enemy—modern war uses but one means: the destruction of the organised forces of the enemy. That destruction is undertaken, prepared, by battle, which overthrows the enemy, disorganises his command, his discipline, his tactical connections and his troops as a force. It is carried out by the pursuit, in the course of which the victor utilises the moral superiority which victory provides over the vanquished, and tears to pieces, finishes off, troops already demoralised, disorganised, no longer manageable–that is, forces which are no longer ...'

On the other hand, if defensive tactics were used rather than offensive, everything would have to happen again. There would be a negative result: 'All this reasoning leads to striking one supreme stroke on one point ... an intentional, resolute, sudden and violent action of the masses on a selected point.'

The firepower of the opposing defenders can be overcome by making use of cover and by the use of artillery: 'It is only when preceded by shells which break obstacles and silence the fire of enemy guns, that infantry will manage to move even in small numbers along its avenues of approach.' But Foch disastrously underestimated the ability of the defenders to withstand this artillery 'softening': 'A quarter of an hour's quick fire by a mass of artillery on a clearly determined objective will generally suffice.' Once this softening has been done, Foch continues, the infantry should advance, firing as they went: 'any rush forward must be preceded by a storm of bullets designed to shake the enemy, in any case to getting him to ground ... to run away or to fall on, such is the unavoidable dilemma (of the attacking forces). To fall on, but to fall on in numbers and masses—therein lies salvation ... march straight on to the goal ... The consideration of what fire one may oneself receive now becomes a secondary matter; the troops are on the move and must arrive ... (59)'

When it all actually happened, in the trenches of World War One, it was almost exactly opposite to what Foch said it would be. Hour upon hour of artillery bombardment failed to break the defences. And at the Somme, rather than 'the troops are on the move and must arrive', Britain alone lost fifteen men killed and thirty men wounded each minute for a period of twenty-four hours.

But Foch had a strong influence before the war. His followers included Colonel de Grandmaison, chief of the operations branch of the general staff, who believed the military leaders shouldn't stop to think too much. They should just attack. He said: 'In the offensive, imprudence is the best safeguard. The least caution destroys all its efficacy.'

Foch's faith in the offensive became, in an exaggerated form, the guiding impulse in the French plan in 1913; Plan XVII had one fixed objective: 'Whatever the circumstances, it is the ... intention

77

to advance, with all forces, to the attack (60).'

Clausewitz had been twisted to the ultimate, not only in France, but throughout the armies of Europe. Mass offensives were the answer. And victory would go to he who attacked first.

Clausewitz: pre-emptive strike

This false interpretation of Clausewitz is illustrated by the introduction to an English translation of *On War* by Colonel F. N. Maude in 1908: '... following out the principles of Clausewitz, victory can only be ensured by the creation in peace of an organisation which will bring every available man, horse, and gun (or ship and gun, if the war be on the sea) in the shortest possible time, and with the utmost possible momentum, upon the decisive field of action—which in turn leads to the final doctrine formulated by Von der Goltz in excuse for the action of the late President Kruger in 1899: "The Statesman who, knowing his instrument to be ready, and seeing War inevitable, hesitates to strike first is guilty of a crime against his country..." (61)'

Meanwhile the Germans were busy preparing their offensive operational schemes. Chief among these was the famous Schlieffen Plan, more correctly a series of plans drawn up by Schlieffen, Chief of the General Staff, between 1897 and 1905.

The Germans were still bedevilled by the problem of how to deal with a war on two fronts, one in the east against Russia, one in the west against France, should those two join together to defeat Germany. Both could not be dealt with at the same time; one would have to be defeated as rapidly as possible, then, making use of Germany's interior lines, forces would have to be switched across to face the other.

However, according to Schlieffen: '... Germany (would have) the advantage of lying between France and Russia and of separating these allies ... Germany must strive, therefore, first, to strike down one of the allies while the other is kept occupied; but then, when the one antagonist is conquered, it must, by exploiting its railroads, bring a superiority of numbers to the other theatre of war, which will also destroy the other enemy... (62)'

Schlieffen's Plan

But prospects for a quick victory against Russia faded, and so, from 1892 onwards, Schlieffen based his plans on defeating France first.

79

Facing page Marshal Foch of France

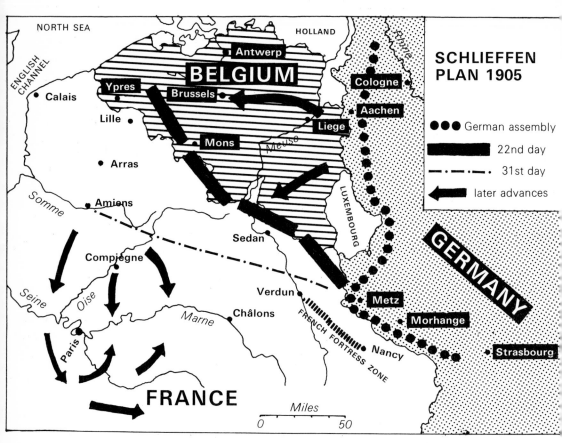

Map illustrating the Schlieffen Plan

'The whole of Germany must hurl itself against one opponent, the one who is the strongest, most powerful, most dangerous; this cannot but be France–England. Austria need feel no anxiety. The Russian army, destined to serve against Germany, will not march on Galicia before the die has been cast in the west, and the fate of Austria will be decided, not on the Bug, but on the Seine (63).'

Schlieffen rightly saw that mass warfare had made the frontal attack difficult. According to his biographer: 'Weapons and military methods—wrote Schlieffen—have entirely changed in two thousand years. The basic conditions of battle remain unchanged ... The target of the main attack is not the enemy front ... The essential is to crush in the flanks ... Annihilation is completed by an attack on the enemy rear (64).'

So, to carry out this theory, he evolved a plan which would make use of railways and mass armies to bring about a Cannae encirclement victory over the French—ignoring the fact that the victor of Cannae was defeated in the end. He concentrated his thoughts on outflanking and advancing behind the French fort system. To do this the Germans could either attempt a push south through Switzerland, or north through Belgium. But Switzerland was easily defended and the country difficult. Yet Belgium would be neutral, and a violation of this neutrality would probably bring Britain into the war.

Schlieffen struggled with this dilemma until 1905. By then he had decided Belgium would have to be invaded. The chance of Britain joining against Germany would have to be taken; if she did, Schlieffen was confident the outcome would still be the same. He then elaborated his Belgian invasion plan in great detail.

'The mass of the western force—seven armies with 69 divisions, counting front line and reserve, 8 cavalry divisions, 22 "Landwehr" (territorial) brigades—was to concentrate in the Rhine Province, with sections also in Lorraine on the Saar. For the decisive offensive they were to advance first against the Dunkirk–Verdun line in a vast leftward wheel with Metz as its pivot, the 8 "Ersatz" army corps were to follow as soon as they were available. In Lorraine only one army was to be retained with 10 divisions, counting front line and reserve, 3 cavalry divisions, 1 "Landwehr" brigade, apart from the war-time garrisons of Metz and Strasbourg. On the upper Rhine only $3\frac{1}{2}$ "Landwehr" brigades were to remain. Upper Alsace was to be left undefended. The relative strengths of the right and left wings of the army in front line and reserve divisions was approximately 7:1 (65).'

But many risks were involved. A heavy weight of German troops in the north would leave few for the south, where the French could attack and penetrate into undefended south Germany; there would

81

be few reserves to protect communications; everything had to work smoothly or all would collapse; in the years before the war Italian help on the upper Rhine, on which Schlieffen had counted, could no longer be considered likely. Schlieffen himself had growing doubts.

The younger Moltke, nephew of the Moltke who had led Germany to victory in 1870, was even more apprehensive. And this successor to Schlieffen not only changed the ratio of German forces in the north and south from 7:1 to 3:1, but he made the whole operation partly dependent on what the French did, on the enemy's will, so introducing additional uncertainty which could not be planned beforehand.

The German plan of 1914 was not therefore the Schlieffen Plan. But like it, it was considered by Germany to be infallible. Statesmen had a misplaced confidence in it. Above all, both the Schlieffen Plan and Moltke's revised version meant that once mobilised, Germany would have to go to war—and against France, even if the threat to Germany was not coming primarily from France but Russia. The plan was geared to attacking westwards first, and could not be changed.

These complicated links between the threats from Russia and France are shown in a memorandum discussing German war preparations, sent by Moltke to Conrad, the Austrian Chief of Staff, in 1909: '... it is extremely doubtful if that country (France) which possesses an army almost equal in numbers to the German armed strength could tolerate a mobilised Germany on her frontiers without herself mobilising. But two mobilised armies, such as the German and French will not be able to face each other without fighting.'

He was uncertain about the treaties between the two:

'It is outside my knowledge how far the agreements into which France has entered oblige her to give active help to Russia in a military conflict between the latter and Germany. That such agreements exist I regard as certain, since present-day Europe is so much shot through and through and interwoven with mutual agreements, "ententes", and alliances, that scarcely any of the European Great Powers can draw the sword without the obligation arising for the one Power to attack the other over the whole continent.'

But:

'I therefore think that if Germany mobilises against Russia, she must also reckon on a war with France... (66)'

Only a month later, the German Kaiser, in full agreement with his Chief of Staff Moltke, wrote in a marginal note to a telegram from his Ambassador in Vienna, Tschirschky: 'France must be told clearly that in the case of a *démarche* of Russia against Austria, the *casus foederis* will arise for us, that means mobilisation. France must give a clear undertaking that she will in no case go to war with us, either at the beginning of the war or later. A declaration of neutrality is not enough. If France refuses us this declaration her refusal will be regarded by us as a *casus belli* ... In no case can the army allow itself to be placed in a situation in which it would engage itself half against Russia and half as a cover against an uncertain France. We must stake all against the west or all against the east (67).'

The complex, and fatal, nature of the German mobilisation plan was brought out in the final hours of peace, 1914, when the Kaiser had a last minute change of heart and wanted Russia, and not France, to be attacked first. Moltke argued this was impossible; the plans were too rigid to be altered; the most that could be done was for the initial mobilisation to be against France, and then, with the troops now organised, for there to be a switch to Russia: '... I assured His Majesty that this was not possible (the idea of attacking Russia first). The deployment of an army of a million men was not a matter of improvisation. It was the product of a whole heavy year's work and, once worked out, could not be changed. If His Majesty insisted on leading the whole army eastwards, he would not have an army ready to strike, he would have a confused mass of disorderly armed men without commissariat ... a mobilised Germany and a mobilised France could not possibly come to an agreement to leave each other alone ... I finally managed to persuade His Majesty that our concentration of strong forces against France and light defensive forces against Russia must be carried out as planned unless the most unholy muddle was to be created. I told the Kaiser that,

Impossible to Attack Russia (1914)

83

once the concentration had been carried out, it would be possible to transfer forces at will to the eastern front, but that concentration itself must proceed unchanged, or else I could not be responsible for things (68).'

Because mobilisation was all part of the operational offensive, troops would be mobilising, deploying, and attacking all at the same time. The railway timetable for the movement westwards was rigid; the programme, once started, couldn't be halted. It would even be difficult to carry out full mobilisation in Germany alone; there simply wasn't sufficient room. Enemy territory had to be taken to gain the necessary space. So, while other countries could mobilise as a form of diplomatic signal, without even intending to fight, a German mobilisation was a declaration war had begun and couldn't be stopped.

Germany was supremely confident the plan would work. The French had similar trust in their own. Both relied on the rapid offensive. Both countries believed they could win the war quickly and cleanly, their armies sweeping to complete victory over all defensive obstacles and backed by the resources of the entire nation in arms.

Indeed, it was realised that victory must come quickly, or the nation would collapse under the strain of supporting the huge war machine; thus Schlieffen believed: '... in an age in which the existence of nations is based on the uninterrupted progress of trade and commerce ... A strategy of exhaustion is impossible when the maintenace of millions necessitates the expenditure of milliards... (69)'

THE ANGLO–GERMAN NAVAL RACE

Britain could remain to a certain extent isolated from the European arms race while she had clear command of the sea. Until the end of the nineteenth century there was no serious rival for this naval supremacy, and Britain was able to maintain her 'two-Power

Standard', ie the British navy should have adequate superiority over the next two strongest Powers, in those days France and Russia. The German navy was considered a harmless hobby of the Kaiser, and until 1896 he received little support from the Reichstag for his desire for a more powerful naval force.

Then, in 1897, Admiral Alfred von Tirpitz became head of the German Navy. In 1898 the vigorous Admiral, helped by the growing feeling among German politicians that Germany could better stand up to Britain's colonial ambitions if she had a more powerful naval force, had the first building programme approved. Another Naval Law followed in early 1900, with Tirpitz saying Germany should be prepared for 'a battle in the North Sea against England'. *German Naval Policy*

The official German reasons for a stronger navy were: '... In order to protect German trade and commerce under existing conditions, only one thing will suffice, namely, Germany must possess a battle fleet of such a strength that, even for the most powerful naval adversary, a war would involve such risks as to make that Power's own supremacy doubtful.

'For this purpose it is not absolutely necessary that the German Fleet should be as strong as that of the greatest naval Power, for, as a rule, a great naval Power will not be in a position to concentrate all its forces against us. Even if it were successful in bringing against us a much superior force, the defeat of a strong German fleet would so considerably weaken the enemy that, in spite of the victory that might be achieved, his own supremacy would no longer be assured by a fleet of sufficient strength ... (70)'

In Britain, disquiet was increasing. Then, in 1904, Britain formed a new home fleet with a base at Rosyth, Scotland. Germany, in 1905, replied with a supplementary naval law. Britain reacted more strongly. In 1905 the keel of the first British Dreadnought was laid at Portsmouth and she began sea trials in 1906. It was believed this one warship, faster than any other, with ten 12 inch guns instead of four, equal to any two of her predecessors on broadside firing or to three firing ahead, could sink the entire Germany navy alone.

The Dreadnought programme was only started after intense

debate, surrounded by the 'big ship' or 'small ship' controversy. *Admiral*The former school won, and in both Britain and Germany a decisive *Mahan* influence was cast by an American naval theorist, Mahan, who argued for bigger, better and more powerful navies.

Mahan's *The Influence of Sea Power upon History, 1660–1783* was published in 1890. It was immediately described as 'the Bible for the big-ship school'. In it, and in subsequent books and articles, he preached control of the sea through concentration of superior force. Great fleets should be powerful rather than fast. They should seek out the enemy and destroy him; the British had defeated the French in the Seven Years' War, for example, because wherever possible 'their studied policy was to assail and destroy their enemy'.

In an article in *Harper's New Monthly*, October 1895, he wrote: 'War, however defensive in moral character, must be waged aggressively if it is to hope for success.' In peace, navies should be built ready for war: 'A navy, therefore, whose primary sphere of action is war, is ... a political factor of the utmost importance in international affairs, one more often a deterrent than irritant.' Mahan refused to accept that torpedo boats posed a risk to battleships. In 1906, describing the lessons to be learnt from the Russo–Japanese War in an article in *The U.S. Naval Institute Proceedings*, he said: 'The experience of this war has confirmed the use and supremacy of the battleship ... the torpedo vessel has achieved less than was expected ... it has come in at the end of the battle ...'

Mahan's influence was enormous. He came at just the right time for the 'big-ship school' and his writings fitted perfectly into the current climate of debate. In 1893 the Kaiser said in a telegram to Poultney Bigelow: 'I am just now not reading but devouring Captain Mahan's book; and am trying to learn it by heart. It is a first class book and classical in all points. It is on board all my ships and constantly quoted by my Captains and officers.'

In 1894, Gladstone resigned. He had disagreed with the proposal to accelerate the naval building programme; and Mahan wrote to his wife: 'Some say that not his eyes only, but his unwillingness to increase naval expenditure caused his retirement, when he found

Facing page The Anglo-German naval race, *top two* the battleship *Kaiser* and cruiser *Moltke, bottom two* H.M.S. *Iron Duke* and H.M.S. *Lion*

his colleagues set upon it. If so, I had a hand in his resignation for all agree in telling me that the increased vote of the navy was due to the books (71).'

Germany also began building Dreadnoughts, and in early 1908 another amendment to the German Navy Law was made providing for four of these giant ships each year until 1911, instead of three. Britain on the other hand had only laid down three of these ships in 1907 and only two in 1908. The naval panic broke out. According to Mr Balfour, recently the Prime Minister, speaking on 16 March 1909, Germany would have thirteen Dreadnoughts by 1 April 1911, to Britain's twelve.

The basic principle of Britain's defence was threatened.

A statement by McKenna, First Lord of the Admiralty, to the Committee of Imperial Defence, 29 May 1911, set out British naval strategy in time of war: '... The object of the Imperial Fleet will be to obtain by unity of maritime effort the command of the sea with the least possible delay. By command of the sea we understand keeping the sea open to ourselves at every point, and closing it to the enemy. Keeping the sea open means that we could at any time and everywhere transport our military forces, and that we should be able to continue our commerce in war almost as well as we can in peace. Closing the sea to the enemy means that not only the shores of these islands, but, with the exception of Canada, all the Dominions would be free from fear of invasion, and the trade of the Empire would be secure. The enemy, on the other hand, would neither be able to transport his forces nor continue his trade, and the result of the economic pressure of the destruction of overseas trade in almost any modern state would be so serious as I believe to constitute something even more than a crippling blow.'

'On the outbreak of War our problem, which will be one and the same all the whole world over, would be to seek out, to bring to battle, or to mask the enemy fleet and enemy cruisers wherever they might be found. And, further, whatever the distribution of our fleet may be, which must be determined by the distribution of the enemy's forces, there is the same Imperial interest affecting us

British Naval Strategy

89

Facing page above H.M.S. *Dreadnought* and *below* a dreadnought squadron in cruising order

all alike, to protect Imperial trade wherever it may be found ... (72)'

Because she had this command of the seas, Britain could afford to do without a large conscript army, relying instead on a small professional force mainly deployed on world-wide imperial duties, rather than having to be garrisoned at home for the defence of this country.

Lord Haldane, Secretary of State for War, made a statement to the Committee of Imperial Defence, 30 May 1911, on the structure and function of the British Army: '... People are fond of speaking of the small British Army, and so it is very small if you take what is at home; but they might just as well speak of the enormous British Army, because it is enormous in another aspect compared with what Germany possesses, for instance. We are an island; we are surrounded by the sea, and it has been our tradition to look to sea power, not only for carrying our troops over the seas, but for protecting these islands. The result is that our defences have been very different from those of other countries. If we were like Germany and France, with land frontiers over which a neighbouring army could mobilise and come at once, we should no doubt have resorted long ago to compulsory service and put every citizen through a period of training, which would enable us to produce an enormous citizen army, a short range weapon to operate only for a very short time to repel invasion; but that has not been our main problem, because we have no land frontiers. We have sea frontiers which we can defend better and more cheaply, relying largely on the navy for the purpose. We have concentrated our strength on producing an overseas army or a set of overseas armies which are for the defence of India, which are for the defence of Africa, and which are for the formation of the Egyptian and Mediterranean garrisons ... (73)'

In fact, by May 1911, the Germans only had five Dreadnoughts completed. But Tirpitz continued his aggressive speeches; Germany should have a navy strong enough to make conflict a dangerous risk for Britain

A speech by Winston Churchill, First Lord of the Admiralty,

91

Facing page King George V of England in his uniform as Admiral of the Fleet

made at Glasgow, February 1912, showed British fears:

He said: 'The purposes of British naval power are essentially defensive. We have no thoughts, and we have never had any thoughts of aggression, and we attribute no such thoughts to other great powers. There is, however, this difference between the British naval power and the naval power of the great and friendly Empire—and I trust it may long remain the great and friendly Empire—of Germany. The British Navy is to us a necessity and, from some points of view, the German Navy is to them more in the nature of a luxury. Our naval power involves British existence. It is existence to us; it is expansion to them. We cannot menace the peace of a single Continental hamlet, no matter how great and supreme our Navy may become. But, on the other hand, the whole fortunes of our race and Empire, the whole treasure accumulated during so many centuries of sacrifice and achievement, would perish and be swept utterly away if our naval supremacy were to be impaired. It is the British Navy which makes Great Britain a great power. But Germany was a great Power respected and honoured all over the world, before she had a single ship... (74)'

It was in the North Sea that Britain believed the most serious German threat would arise; Churchill told the Committee of Imperial Defence on 11 July 1912: '... I think I am justified in saying that the German fleet, whatever may be said about it, exists for the purpose of fighting a great battle in the North Sea, both with battleships and with all ancillary vessels, against some other great Naval Power which is not referred to by them... (75)'

In 1912 another German Navy Law was passed, with Tirpitz believing Germany would eventually win the spiralling naval race because of her cheaper construction costs, and her ability to man the increasing number of warships with conscript sailors.

Britain managed to keep the lead, but she was indeed feeling the strain. To keep the superiority in home waters, warships had to be brought back from the Far East and also from the Mediterranean. The result of the withdrawals from the latter meant Britain had to depend more on the French: French ships would protect British interests in the Mediterranean while Britain did the same for France

Facing page above the crew of the German cruiser *Moltke*, and *below* the Duke of York inspecting the British navy at Portsmouth

in the North Sea. Tirpitz believed this to be a triumph for his policy.

Writing later he said: '... In order to estimate the strength of the trump card which our fleet put in the hands of an energetic diplomacy at this time, one must remember that in consequence of the concentration of the English forces which we had caused in the North Sea, the English control of the Mediterranean and Far-Eastern waters had practically ceased (76).'

He also believed Germany's increased naval strength had made Britain more 'respectful'; '... British statesmen naturally did not stress the fact in their conversations with Germans that it was mainly the presence of our own nearly completed fleet in the North Sea that had produced their respectful tone, and had lessened the probability of a British attack ... seventeen years of fleet building had ... improved the prospects of an acceptable peace with England (77).'

Bethmann Hollweg declared after the war: 'Sea power cast a spell that many a critic even of the smallest item in the budget could not resist. And in the country the further you were from the

German Naval Romance

coast the brighter glittered the sea in the light of romance. The fleet was the pet of Germany, and seemed to embody the energies and enthusiasms of the nation ... The doubts of a small circle of experts as to whether we were on the right lines in building capital ships at all, could make no headway against a fanatical journalism wholly in the service of the prevailing policy. Questionings as to the grave internationl embarrassments caused us by our naval policy were shouted down by a boisterous agitation ... The direction of the fleet had lain for years in the hands of a man (Tirpitz) who had arrogated to himself a political authority far beyond his functions, and who had a lasting influence on the political point of view of an important circle. Whenever an issue arose between the naval authorities and the political administration, the public almost invariably supported the former (78).'

The German attitude was summed up by the Kaiser's reaction at the end of 1911 to an article in the *Westminster Gazette* headed

Kaiser on England

'Towards an Anglo–German Détente'. He read it and then jotted down these notes: 'Quite good, except for the ridiculous insinuation that we are aspiring after the hegemony in Central Europe. We simply *are* Central Europe ... To this the British object, because it absolutely knocks to pieces their theory of the "Balance of Power", ie their desire to be able to play off one European Power against another at their own pleasure, and because it would lead to the establishment of a united Continent—a contingency which they want to prevent at all costs ...'

A powerful German navy would hinder Britain's power game, believed the Kaiser, and in addition, as he wrote to Ballin, the General Director of the Hamburg–America Steamship Company, in December 1912: 'I as you know have always looked upon Great Britain as an enemy in a military sense (79).'

But in fact this new dependence of Britain on France, and likewise for France on Britain, meant the two countries were bound more closely. It meant that if France were attacked, Britain would have greater difficulty in not getting involved. Britain was getting dragged into European problems; and for the first time, with the growth of other navies, Britain was also being directly threatened.

In a memorandum of January 1914 Winston Churchill, First Lord of the Admiralty, put it like this: '... Besides the Great Powers, there are so many small States who are buying or building great ships of war, and whose vessels may by some diplomatic combination, or by duress, be brought into the line against us. None of these Powers need, like us, navies to defend their actual safety or independence. They build them so as to play a part in the world's affairs. It is sport to them. It is death to us ... *Churchill: Naval Escalation*

'... Although (during the past year) the foundations of peace among the Great Powers have been strengthened, the causes which might lead to a general war have not been removed ... There has not been the slightest abatement of naval and military preparation. On the contrary, we are witnessing this year increases of expenditure by the Continental Powers beyond all previous experience. The world is arming as it has never armed before. Every suggestion of arrest or limitation has been brushed aside (80).'

4 Summer 1914: One Crisis Too Many

ON 28 JUNE 1914, Archduke Franz Ferdinand, heir to the Hapsburg throne, was visiting Sarajevo, capital of Bosnia. The Archduke, a field marshal and Inspector-General of the Austro–Hungarian army, wished to inspect his troops. One personal reason for his visit was that he wanted to take the opportunity for his wife to ride beside him in an open car on an official occasion. Franz Ferdinand had married beneath him. His wife, Countess Sophie Chotek, was not allowed, because of the rules and restrictions of his rank, to sit beside him on public occasions except when he was acting in a military capacity.

The Archduke was unpopular among the leaders of the Austro–Hungarian empire for other reasons than his ill-advised marriage. The Magyar nobles were certain he intended to break their power in the Monarchy by introducing universal suffrage in Hungary when he became king, and, ironically as it happened, that he also had plans to create a third kingdom for the South Slavs. Ferdinand was opposed to the plans of the party led by Conrad von Hötzendor, Chief of the Austro–Hungarian General Staff, which maintained the Serbian problem could only be solved by war.

But on this day, 28 June, Ferdinand was killed, and by Slavs or Slav sympathisers. The account of his assassination is well-known: the unsuccessful attempt by Austrian schoolboys; Ferdinand angry because his wife's day had been spoilt; the chauffeur taking the wrong turning and having to stop to reverse; Gavrilo Princip, one of the schoolboys, just happening to be there at that time on his way home, and with the perfect opportunity offered, firing the two

97

Facing page above and middle Archduke Ferdinand and his wife minutes before being shot, *below* the arrest of the assassin Princip

shots which killed Sophie and Ferdinand—and which started the final slide downwards to the First World War.

The assassination had been carried out by Austrians, but they had been armed and trained in Serbia by the Black Hand secret society, also called 'Unity or Death', and formed in May 1911 with the hard-core recruited from among Serbian regular army officers.

Colonel Dimitrijevic, one of the founders of Black Hand, said later: '... feeling that Austria–Hungary was making preparations for war against us, I thought that with the disappearance of Franz Ferdinand, the party and the climate of opinion he represented would lose its impetus, and that the danger of war would thus be removed, or at any rate postponed, from Serbia... (81)'

But there was no proof of complicity by the Serbian Government itself. On 14 July von Wiesner, sent from Vienna to Sarajevo to examine the records taken at the inquiry into the assassination, reported: '... Nothing proves complicity of the Serbian Government in carrying out the attack, or in its preparation or in supply of arms, and it is not even to be presumed. There are, on the contrary, indications that give reason to consider such complicity as non-existent (82).'

In the first days after the assassination it seemed that it had not caused a serious crisis. The Russian Ambassador to Vienna reported: '... The tragic end of Archduke Franz-Ferdinand found little response in financial circles here and on the stock-exchange—this index of the mood in business circles. The value of government stocks did not change, which is explained here by confidence in the continuation of peace... (83)'

But, significantly, the reason and the opportunity for Austria to humiliate Serbia was now there; and many Austrians believed opportunities to do this in the past had been missed. In the two weeks after the assassination discussions took place in Vienna to decide how best the humiliation could be brought about, and there was overwhelming support for firm diplomatic action, backed by a show of military strength—and possibly even a limited military operation.

And so an ultimatum Note was prepared, written in extremely

harsh and demanding terms.

These closing passages of the ultimatum, although exaggerated, *The Austrian* were not in fact entirely incorrect: '... The history of the last *Ultimatum* few years and the sad events of 28 June have proved the existence of a subversive movement in Serbia, the aim of which is the detachment of certain territories from Austro–Hungary.

'This movement, which originated in the full view of the Serbian Government, found its expression on this side of the frontier in a number of terrorist acts. The Serbian Government not only did not respect the formal obligations of the declaration of 31 March 1909, it did nothing to suppress this movement... (84)'

According to Sir Edward Grey: '... (he had) never before seen one State address to another independent State a document of so formidable a character... (85)'

Berlin not only promised support, but urged the Austrians on, believing them to be irresolute.

Action against Serbia seems now to have been bound to cause a clash between European powers and almost inevitable war. Then, it did not seem so. All the moves and pressures against Serbia, even the Austrian declaration of war which was to come on 26 July, were more diplomatic than military. The Austrian army would not be ready for some weeks. The German Kaiser probably believed the Tzar would feel as he did—that the assassination had been a violation of the position of all Monarchs. Moreover, the Russian war preparations would not be completed until 1917.

Jagow, the German Foreign Secretary, wrote to Lichnowsky, *Russian* Ambassador to London, on 18 July: '... In a few years, according *Military* to all competent authorities, Russia will be ready to strike. Then *Delays* she will crush us with her numbers; then she will have built her Baltic fleet and her strategical railways ... I desire no preventive war. But when battle offers we must not run away (86).'

As Britain had the Irish Home Rule problem to deal with, the time could not have seemed more convenient for the Germans.

As for France, some precaution was taken by the Austrians in *The French* the timing of the ultimatum. The French President, Poincaré, and *Off Guard* Premier Viviani, were at sea, returning from a state visit to Russia, when the Austrian moves were made. The actual delivery of the Note was delayed an hour, to 6.0 p.m., 23 July, to make sure the French leaders were far enough from land. In addition, the ultimatum had only a forty-eight hour time limit, preventing effective consultation between Serbia and Russia.

Poincaré wrote afterwards: '... [we] were steaming through the open Baltic when a wireless message told us that the German Emperor had curtailed his cruise and was on his way back to Kiel. In our floating abode, however, we heard only the drowsy echoes of what was happening in the world outside... (87)'

Meanwhile, until 23 July, all attempts were made in Austria and Germany to give the impression little was to happen; the Kaiser went on holiday for, as Bethmann Hollweg said: '... I had advised him to undertake this journey in order to avoid the attention that would have been aroused by his giving up an outing that he had for years been accustomed to take at this time of year... (88)'

Moltke did the same; the press said Austria's action 'would take the politest form, according to the usual practice.' (*Berliner Lokal-Anzeiger.*) To avoid suspicion, Austria even practised deception on Italy, her nominal ally; the Italians were not allowed to see the Note until 24 July, after it had been delivered.

German Posture Berlin also claimed the Austrians had not fully consulted her, and that Jagow, the German Foreign Minister, was not shown the contents of the Note until the afternoon of 22 July, when it was too late to do anything about it.

Jagow said in a circular dispatch to German Ambassadors on 24 July: 'We have had no influence of any kind on the text of the Note, and we have had no more opportunity than the other Powers to take sides in any way before its publication (89).'

But though this could be called a slight, Berlin probably welcomed the ability to plead ignorance; not having been shown the Note until too late, the Germans could avoid responsibility for the consequences. There is little doubt they had promised full support to the Austrians, and had done so some time before.

Austria Relies on Germany Szögyeny, Austrian Ambassador to Berlin reported to Vienna on 5 July: '... As far as our relations with Serbia are concerned, the German Government's stand-point is that we should judge ourselves what is to be done to clear up the relationship; in this respect, we can rely on Germany as an ally and as a friend, whatever course we take ... The Chancellor, like his Imperial master, regards our immediate intervention against Serbia as the most radical and best solution of our difficulties in the Balkans... (90)'

And the Kaiser himself had written to Ballin in December 1912: *The Kaiser* '... The Slav subjects of Austria had become very restless and could only be brought to reason by resolute action of the whole Dual Monarchy against Serbia ... If we were compelled to take up arms we should do so to assist Austria not only against Russian aggression, but also against the Slavs in general and in her efforts to remain German ... It is beyond our power to prevent this struggle, because the future of the Hapsburg Monarchy and that of our own country are both at stake... (91)'

Despite the harshness of the Note, the Serbs accepted most of Austria's ten demands. The Kaiser believed: '... (it was) a brilliant performance for a time limit of only 48 hours. This is more than one could have expected! A great moral victory for Vienna; but with it every reason for war disappears ... (92)'

But at the same time there were reports of Russian military activity. On 27 July the German Chancellor, Bethmann Hollweg, was informed there were signs of Russian military preparations on the German frontier. The Chancellor advised Vienna to be cautious. But the Austrians refused to accept the Serbian reply to their Note, and ordered partial mobilisation of their army.

Germany did not want widespread war. There is every possibility *Localised* the statements made by the German Ambassadors in St. Peters- *Conflict?* burg, Paris and London to the respective Governments, that Berlin wanted the conflict to be 'localised', were genuine.

They informed Entente capitals that: 'We urgently desire the localisation of the conflict, as the intervention of any other Power would, as a result of the various alliance obligations, bring about inestimable consequences (93).'

Moreover, Moltke knew that if Austria attacked Serbia, even

101

with only part of her army, Russia would be forced to intervene and Austria would have to mobilise the rest of her army against her.

In a memorandum of 28 July Moltke wrote that Austria would not be able to move against Serbia: '... without making Russian intervention certain. That means she will have to mobilise the other half of her army, for she cannot possibly put herself at the mercy of Russia ready for war (94).'

When either Russia or Austria ordered even partial mobilisation, the other, threatened, had to do the same. This meant the generals taking over more control, war machines being inexorably put into motion, diplomatic attempts to avoid the conflict being stifled, and confusion being more widespread.

And this indeed is what happened. Russia, in view of the Austrian threat to Serbia and also to herself, had ordered partial mobilisation on the evening of 20 July. The threat from Austria increased. The Russians therefore ordered general mobilisation on 31 July. Early that same morning Austria also fully mobilised. But it was still bluff and counter-bluff. Neither the Austrian nor the Russian armies were fully ready.

Meanwhile, in London three-quarters of the British Cabinet were opposed to the country being involved. On 24 July, Sir Edward Grey, the Foreign Secretary, had informed the French Ambassador that the Austro–Serbian dispute was of no concern to Britain.

But if France were attacked, Britain could not stand aside. The Entente still existed, although this was not a binding, inflexible commitment.

As late as 31 July, President Poincaré, appealing to King George V for Britain to make clear whether she would intervene to help France in the event of German hostilities, admitted that Britain was not bound to do so: '... Undoubtedly our military and naval engagements leave Your Majesty's Government entirely free, and in the letters exchanged in 1912 between Sir E. Grey and M. Paul Cambon, Great Britain and France are merely pledged the one to the other to conversations in the event of European tension, with a view to considering whether there is ground for common action ... (95)'

Relevance of the Entente: Poincaré

103

Facing page Sir Edward Grey, the British Foreign Secretary

Grey   Yet it would still have been difficult for Britain to avoid entangle-
ment because of it. As Grey said in a secret memorandum in
February 1906: 'If there is a war between France and Germany, it
will be very difficult for us to keep out of it. The "Entente", and still
more constant and emphatic demonstrations of affection (official,
naval, political, commercial, municipal and in the press) have created
in France a belief that we should support her in war ... If this expecta-
tion is disappointed, the French will never forgive us. There would
also, I think, be a general feeling in every country that we had
behaved meanly and left France in the lurch. The United States
would despise us. Russia would not think it worth while to make a
friendly arrangement with us about Asia; Japan would prepare to
re-insure herself elsewhere; we should be left without a friend and
without the power of making a friend, and Germany would take
some pleasure, after what has passed, in exploiting the whole situation to our disadvantage ... (96)'

Churchill   Britain was even more obligated by the 1912 naval dispositions,
with the mutual reliance for protection by Britain and France.
In August 1912, the Cabinet had decided naval conversations
should take place with France, similar to those started in 1906
between the General Staffs; Churchill was among those who feared
British involvement in a future conflict through close relationships:
'... (consider) how tremendous would be the weapon which France
would possess to compel our intervention, if she could say "on the
advice of and by arrangement with your naval authorities we have
left our Northern coasts defenceless. We cannot possibly come back
in time" (from the Mediterranean). Indeed, it would probably be
decisive whatever is written down now. Every one must feel who
knows the facts that we have the obligations of an alliance without
its advantages ...(97)'

Events quickened in the confused, final, fatal hours of early
August. The tragedy of the effects of the elaborate mobilisation
plans now took place. Because Russia's army was not ready, and
the military reorganisation programme would not be completed
until 1917, she could not mobilise against Austria without being
inadequately defended against an attack from Austria's ally,

Germany. To provide this defence, there had to be the full mobilisation of her entire forces. But this meant Germany also felt threatened, and in addition, with Austria mobilised, Germany was bound to support her. On 31 July, Bethmann Hollweg asked Moltke, the German Chief of Staff, if Germany was in danger from the Russian mobilisation. Moltke, with the belief shared by all the major European military leaders that the country which struck first would win, answered yes. Germany sent an ultimatum, demanding Russian demobilisation. Russia, knowing this would leave her defenceless, refused. On 1 August, Germany therefore declared war on Russia.

But under the rigid German operational plans, if action were to be taken against Russia, it would have to be taken first against France. Belgium would be invaded, so bringing Britain into the war. Moreover, Germany had to move rapidly in order to use the war plan effectively. *German War Plans*

Bethmann Hollweg described the situation in Berlin: 'We were not in complete agreement among ourselves as to how we were to proceed officially. The War Minister, General von Falkenhayn, thought it was a mistake to declare war on Russia, because he feared that the political effect would be prejudicial to us. The Chief of the General Staff, General von Moltke, was on the other hand in favour of declaring war ... because our hope of success ... was dependent on the extreme rapidity of our movement. I myself agreed with the view of General von Moltke ...(98)'

For a few hours some hope still remained of Britain not being involved. It seemed Britain would stand aside if France were not attacked. Moltke wrote: '... On the day before mobilisation (of the German army) a dispatch arrived from London, in which it was stated that England had given an undertaking to France to protect her against German attack from the sea against her northern coast. The Kaiser asked me for my opinion, and I said that we could unhesitatingly give a guarantee not to attack the northern coast of France if England would, on this understanding, agree to remain neutral ...(99)' *Moltke: Need to Strike*

If such was the case, said the Kaiser, the German thrust should be to the east, against Russia, and not to the west. Moltke was horrified. It couldn't be done: '... I nearly fell into despair. I regarded these diplomatic moves, which threatened to interfere with the carrying out of our mobilisation, as the greatest disaster for the impending war ...(100)' All the detailed, inflexible plans for mobilisation called for the westwards movement. As it was, Moltke was relieved to find there had been an apparent misunderstanding of Britain's attitude. So the invasion of Belgium would still take place, even if Britain did join the war as a result.

British Precautions

It is hardly surprising that the position of England was uncertain if Sir Edward Grey could tell the German Ambassador as late as 1 August: 'Our hands are still free. Our attitude will be determined largely—I will not say entirely—by the question of Belgium, which appeals very strongly to public opinion here (101).'

However, Britain was already increasing navy precautions. A telegram went from First Lord to the Fleets, 27 July: 'This is not the Warning Telegram, but European political situation makes war between Triple Entente and Triple Alliance Powers by no means impossible. Be prepared to shadow possible hostile men-of-war and consider dispositions of H.M. ships under your command from this point of view. Measure is purely precautionary. No unnecessary person to be informed. The utmost secrecy to be observed (102).'

British Naval Measures

It was also significant that on 28 July, instead of dispersing after manoeuvres, the Royal Navy's main fleet was ordered to remain concentrated: in effect this was the first move towards mobilisation.

'BRITISH NAVAL MEASURES

ORDERS TO FIRST AND SECOND FLEETS

NO MANOEUVRE LEAVE

'We received the following statement from the Secretary of the Admiralty at an early hour this morning:

'Orders have been given to the First Fleet, which is concentrated at Portland, not to disperse for manoeuvre leave for the present. All vessels of the Second Fleet are remaining at their home ports in proximity to their balance crews ...(103)'

Then, at 6.20 p.m., 28 July, the German Naval Attaché's telegram from London was received in Berlin: 'Admiralty are not publishing

Facing page The German Imperial Staff with General von Moltke in the foreground

ships' movements. Second Fleet remains fully manned. Schools closed in naval bases; preliminary measures taken for recall from leave. According to unconfirmed news First Fleet still at Portland, one submarine flotilla left Portsmouth. It is to be assumed that Admiralty is preparing for mobilisation on the quiet (104).'

From the Admiralty a telegram to Commander-in-Chief Home Fleets, sent 5 p.m., 28 July: 'Tomorrow, Wednesday, the First Fleet is to leave Portland for Scapa Flow. Destination is to be kept secret except to flag and commanding officers...(105)'

On 2 August, Berlin demanded free passage through Belgium in order to get to France. This was refused. On 3 August, Germany declared war on France using, as an excuse, the alleged threat to Germany of French troop concentration near the frontier, and blaming the Entente powers for the existing state of affairs. *German Declaration of War*

An almost incredible confusion surrounded the drafting and sending of a declaration of war on France; a draft made on 1 August was not used, instructions telegraphed to Schoen, Ambassador to Paris, were garbled in transit, there were arguments about what reasons should be given for declaring war, and conflicting reports of violation of Belgian territory by French troops, and of shooting incidents. Schoen eventually saw the French Prime Minister on the evening of 3 August and read the following document: 'The German administrative and military authorities have established a certain number of flagrantly hostile acts committed on German territory by French military airmen. Several of these latter have openly violated the neutrality of Belgium by flying over the territory of that country. One of them has attempted to destroy buildings near Wesel, others have been seen over the Eifel region, another dropped bombs on the railway near Karlsruhe and Nuremberg.

'I am instructed and have the honour to inform Your Excellency that in the presence of these acts of aggression the German Empire considers itself in a state of war with France in consequence of the acts of this latter Power ...(106)'

The Kaiser was to write after the war: '... The Treaty directed against Germany—sometimes called the "Gentleman's agreement" of the spring of 1897—is the basis, the point of departure, for this *The Kaiser's Version*

Facing page Winston Churchill in 1912 as First Lord of the Admiralty

war which was systematically developed by the Entente countries for seventeen years. When they had succeeded in winning over Russia and Japan for their purpose, they struck the blow, after Serbia had staged the Sarajevo murder, and had thus touched the match to the carefully filled powder barrel ...(107)'

Bethmann Hollweg

Bethmann Hollweg told the Reichstag in August 1915: '... King Edward VII believed that his principal task was to isolate Germany. The encirclement by the Entente with openly hostile tendencies was drawn closer year by year ...(108)'

On 3 August the Belgian King made a direct appeal for British and French aid. The overwhelming majority of British Ministers were now united on the need to support Britain's allies.

Grey addresses Parliament

Sir Edward Grey made a long speech to the House of Commons on the afternoon of 3 August in which he outlined Britain's position: '... I have put to the House and dwelt at length upon how vital is the condition of the neutrality of Belgium. What other policy is there before the House? There is but one way in which the Government could make certain at the present moment of keeping outside this war, and that would be that it should immediately issue a proclamation of unconditional neutrality. We cannot do that. We have made the commitment to France that I have read to the House ... The Belgian Treaty obligations, the possible position in the Mediterranean, with damage to British interests, and what may happen to France from our failure to support France—if we were to say that all these things nothing mattered ... we should, I believe, sacrifice our respect and good name and reputation before the world, and should not escape the most serious and grave economic consequences ... We believe we shall have the support of the House at large in proceeding to whatever the consequences may be ... I have put the vital facts before the House, and if, as seems not improbable, we are forced, and rapidly forced, to take our stand upon these issues, then I believe, when the country realises what is at stake, what the real issues are, the magnitude of the impending dangers in the West of Europe, which I have endeavoured to describe to the House, we shall be supported throughout, not only by the House of Commons, but by the determination, the resolution, the courage, and the endurance of the whole country (109).'

The *Times* leader, 3 August, stated what many now felt:

THE GERMAN INVASION

'The die is cast. The great European struggle which the nations have so long struggled to avert has begun. Germany declared war upon Russia on Saturday evening, and yesterday her troops entered Luxemburg and crossed the French frontier in Lorraine without any declaration at all. It is idle to dwell upon events such as these. They speak for themselves in a fashion which all can understand. They mean that Europe is to be the scene of the most terrible war that she has witnessed since the fall of the Roman Empire. The losses in human life and in the accumulated wealth of generations which such a contest must involve are frightful to think on. That it should have come about despite the zealous efforts of diplomacy and against the wishes of almost all the nations whom it is destined to afflict, is a grim satire upon the professions of peace yet fresh upon the lips of those who have plunged the Continent into its miseries and its calamities.

'Germany is shown to be at fault:

'The blame must fall mainly upon Germany. She could have stayed the plague had she chosen to speak in Vienna as she speaks when she is in earnest. She has not chosen to do so. She has preferred to make demands in St. Petersburg and in Paris which no Government could entertain, and to defeat by irrevocable acts the last efforts of this country and of others for mediation. She has lived up to the worst principles of the Frederician tradition—the tradition which disregards all obligations of right and wrong at the bidding of immediate self-interest. She believes that her admirable military organisation has enabled her to steal a march upon her rivals. She has been mobilising in all but name, while her mobilisation has been retarded by the 'conversations' she continued until her moment had come. Then she flung the mask aside. While her Ambassador was still in Paris, while by the customs traditional with all civilised peoples she was still at peace with France, she has sent her soldiers

111

into Luxemburg, and invaded the territory of the Republic. It is hard to say which of these acts is the grosser infringement of public right. With Luxemburg she makes no pretence of quarrel. She is herself a party to the guarantee of its neutrality contained in the Treaty of 1867. The other guarantors are Great Britain, France, Russia, Italy, Austria–Hungary, Belgium and the Netherlands. She solemnly pledged herself with some of them, including France and ourselves, to respect this neutrality.'

She is now to be distrusted:

'The world sees how Germany keeps her word. She has been weak enough, or cynical enough, to issue an explanation of her breach of faith. Let Englishmen, who have been disposed to trust her, judge it for themselves. She has not, she says, committed a hostile act by crossing the frontiers, by forcibly interrupting the telephonic communication. These are merely measures to protect the railways for a possible attack by the French. For the sudden invasion of France no excuse has yet been published. When it does it will doubtless be of about equal worth (110).'

On the morning of 4 August, German troops crossed the Belgian frontier. That day Britain sent an ultimatum to Germany to stop the invasion.

British Naval Telegrams A telegram Admiralty to all ships, went out 4 August, 2.5 p.m.: 'The British ultimatum to Germany will expire at midnight Greenwich Mean Time, 4 August. No act of war should be committed before that hour, at which time the telegram to commence hostilities against Germany will be dispatched from the Admiralty ...' Telegram from Admiralty, 5.50 p.m.: 'General message. The war telegram will be issued at midnight authorising you to commence hostilities against Germany, but in view of our ultimatum they may decide to open fire at any moment. You must be ready for this (111).'

Declaration of War The ultimatum expired at midnight. Four years of slaughter had begun.

THE DECLARATION OF WAR

'This day will be momentous in the history of all time. Last evening Germany sent a curt refusal to the demand of this country that she, like France, should respect the neutrality of Belgium. Thereupon the BRITISH AMBASSADOR was handed his passports, and a state of war was formally declared by this country ... We have refused to do today what MR GLADSTONE told us in 1870 honour and conscience forbade us to do. We have refused "quietly to stand by and witness the perpetration of the direst crime that ever stained the pages of history, and thus become participators in the sin". We are fighting now to save a flourishing constitutional Kingdom which has constantly deserved and enjoyed our friendship against a wrong no independent State could tolerate without the loss of all its most essential liberties. We are going into the war that is forced upon us as the defenders of the weak and the champions of the liberties of Europe. We are drawing the sword in the same cause for which we drew it against PHILIP II, against LOUIS XIV, and against NAPOLEON. It is the cause of right and honour, but it is also the cause of our own vital and immediate interests. The Netherlands and Belgium largely owe their independent existence to the instinct we have ever felt and ever acted upon—that on no account whatever can England suffer the coasts of the North Sea and of the narrow seas over against her own to be at the command of a great military monarchy, be that monarchy which it may ...

'We must suffer much, but we shall know how to suffer for the great name of England and for all her high ideals, as our fathers did before us. We go into the fray without hatred, without passion, without selfish ambitions or selfish ends ...(112)'

5 Conclusion

NO ONE can say exactly when the war started. There was no real final decision. Instead there was a rapidly accelerating slide down into bloody horror. One factor in this final slide brought another with it. The actions of one country affected those of another. Never had alliances been more entangling.

France was tied to Russia: to defend herself against Germany, she needed the massive manpower which vast Russia could provide. Germany, encircled, needed Austria; while Austria, with a decaying, disintegrating Empire, needed Germany even more. The South Slavs continued to agitate in Austro–Hungary. Serbia continued to be a threat. Germany was therefore bound to an Austria which was being eroded by the crippling forces of nationalism. Russia felt she needed security and a deep sea harbour in the south; Germany felt Russia had to be blocked to provide a gap in the encirclement. Germany and Britain continued the naval race; and Britain felt her security and her Empire depended on continued British supremacy of the seas.

The 'balance of power' had been created; yet really there is no such thing. At the best it is a confused title meaning whatever one wants it to mean. It could describe the existing state of affairs; or the belief that your own side should be stronger; or that the bigger Powers should negotiate together at the expense of the weak.

In 1914 the term 'balance of power' described a complex, artificial edifice composed of different ideas and attitudes and fears. It lacked any form of stability or permanence. It was a shifting mass, a roping

115

Facing page (left to right) the French Generals Foch, d'Arbal and Balfourie watch troops bound for the northern front in February 1915

together of restless horses and riders each seeking to go different ways and yet with reins linking one with the other. Such stability as the balance had was flimsy, able to be shifted one way or another by a slight puff of wind. And such a breath of wind could be provided by any change in the European status quo—or even by the suggestion of such a change. And the whole frail structure was bound up and supported by the iron framework of massive military power which had armed entire nations.

So continuation of European peace, after so long without war, depended upon continuation of the status quo. The balance was enforced by arms rivalry, itself based on a disastrous misconception—the belief in the offensive. There was the tragic paradox: diplomatically, the alliances were intended to be defensive. But the military plans to strengthen these defensive alliances were based on the offensive. What a country did to prevent an attack was the same it did to launch an attack. Neighbouring countries could not distinguish between the two.

The situation was wide open to miscalculation, both militarily and diplomatically. And both statesmen and generals miscalculated; the former in their belief that mobilisation would not necessarily mean war, the latter in their belief that if and when war did come, it could be won quickly and decisively.

Peacetime weapons of bluff and threat had been used successfully before. This time they misfired. And the whole shaky European diplomatic and military structure collapsed with a roar into chaos, each bringing the other with it. Both statesmen and generals were submerged and suffocated by the force and magnitude of the events they had each helped set in motion. Once started, the momentum of war could not be stopped. War became, as Clausewitz had warned it would if it were allowed to run away with itself, 'a senseless thing without object'.

NOTES ON SOURCES

(1) *Readings in Modern European History,* Volume II (Boston, 1909)

(2) Kertesz, *Documents in the Political History of the European Continent, 1815–1939* (Oxford, 1968)

(3) *Ibid*

(4) Churchill, *World Crisis 1911–1918* (Odhams, 1938)

(5) *Documents from the Russian Archives* (1931)

(6) Alp, *Thoughts on the Nature and Plan of a Greater Turkey*

(7) Kiepenheuer, *Turkish and Pan Turkish Ideal* (Weimar, 1915)

(8) *Memoirs of Count Witte* (1921)

(9) Sack, *Birth of the Russian Democracy* (New York, Russian Information Bureau, 1918)

(10) Golder, *Documents of Russian History, 1914–1917* (The Century Press, New York, 1927)

(11) *London Weekly Times* (27th July, 1906)

(12) Vésinier, *History of the Commune of Paris* (London, Chapman and Hall, 1872)

(13) Conybeare, *The Dreyfus Case* (London, Allen, 1898)

(14) Memorandum by Sir Eyre Crowe (1st January, 1907)

(15) Churchill, *World Crisis*

(16) Gwynn, *Life of Redmond* (London, 1932)

(17) Churchill, *World Crisis*

(18) *American Historical Review* (January, 1918)

(19) Albertini, *Origins of the War of 1914,* Volume I (Oxford University Press, 1965)

(20) Chiala, *Tunisi* (Turin, 1895)

(21) *British and Foreign State Papers* Volume *cxxi* (1925)

(22) Pribram, *Secret Treaties of Austria-Hungary, 1879–1914* (Harvard University Press, 1920)

(23) *Ibid*

(24) *Ibid*

(25) Spender, *Fifty Years of Europe: A Study of Pre-War Documents* (New York, 1933)

(26) *New Chapters of Bismarck's Autobiography,* trans. Bernard Miall (Hodder and Stoughton, 1920)

(27) Lutz, *Die europaische Politik in der Julikrise 1914* (1930)

(28) Pribram, *Secret Treaties of Austria-Hungary*

(29) *Die Grosse Politik,* xi, 31 (1923)

(30) Moltke, *Military Testament*

(31) Asquith, *Genesis of The War* (George H. Doran & Co., 1923)

(32) Albertini, Volume I

(33) Asquith, *Genesis of The War*

(34) Paléologue *Un prélude à l'invasion de la Beligique: Le plan Schlieffen* (Paris, 1932)

(35) Albertini, Volume I

(36) *Ibid*

(37) Spender, *Fifty Years of Europe*

(38) Sir Edward Grey, *Twenty-five Years: 1892–1916* (1925)

(39) Sir Sidney Lee, *King Edward VII,* Volume II (1925)

117

(40) Albertini, Volume I
(41) Momcilo Ninčić, *La Crise Bosniaque*, Volume I, (Paris, 1937)
(42) Asquith, *Genesis of The War*
(43) *Danzer's Armee-Zeitung* (7th January, 1909)
(44) Bethmann Hollweg, *Reflections on the World War*
(45) Churchill, *World Crisis*
(46) Albertini, Volume I
(47) *Ibid*
(48) Asquith, *Genesis of The War*
(49) *Foreign Office Statement* (1915)
(50) Asquith, *Genesis of The War*
(51) Conrad von Hotzendorf, *Aus meiner Dienstzeit*, Volume III (Vienna, 1922–5)
(52) Austrian *note verbale* (18th October, 1913)
(53) Albertini, Volume I
(54) French Law of August, 1793
(55) *Memoirs and Letters of Sir Robert Morier: 1826 to 1876* (London, 1911)
(56) Von Moltke, *Gesammelte Schriften und Denkwürdigkeiten* (1891–4)
(57) *Theory and Practice of War*, ed. Michael Howard
(58) *Ibid*
(59) Foch, *Principles of War* (1903)
(60) *Plan XVII* (Paris, 1913)
(61) Clausewitz, *On War*, trans. by J.J.Graham (1908)
(62) Craig, *Politics of the Prussian Army* (Oxford University Press, 1964)
(63) Wolfgang Foerster, *Graf Schlieffen und er Weltkrieg* (1925)
(64) *Ibid*
(65) *Ibid*
(66) Conrad, *Aus meiner Diemstzeit* (Vienna, 1922–5), Volume I
(67) Albertini, Volume I
(68) Moltke, *Erinnerungen, Briefe, Dokumente 1877–1916* (Stuttgart, 1922)
(69) Craig, *Politics of the Prussian Army* (Oxford University Press, 1964)
(70) Preamble to German Navy Law (1900)
(71) Puleston, *Mahan*
(72) Asquith, *Genesis of The War*
(73) *Ibid*
118 (74) Churchill, *World Crisis*

(75) Asquith, *Genesis of The War*
(76) Churchill, *World Crisis*
(77) *Ibid*
(78) Bethmann Hollweg, *Reflections*
(79) B. Huldermann, *Albert Ballin* (Cassell, 1922)
(80) Asquith, *Genesis of The War*
(81) Stoyan Gavrilovic, *Journal of Modern History* (December, 1955)
(82) Asquith, *Genesis of The War*
(83) *Documents from Russian Archives* (Leningrad, 1931)
(84) Zeman, *Break-up of the Hapsburg Empire, 1914–18* (Oxford University Press, 1961)
(85) Grey, *Twenty-Five Years*
(86) Asquith, *Genesis of The War*
(87) Raymond Poincaré, *Au service de la France, Neuf anneés de souvenirs* (Paris, 1926–33)
(88) Bethmann Hollweg, *Reflections*
(89) Bernadotte Schmitt, *Coming of the War*, Volume I (New York, 1930)
(90) Zeman, *Break-up of the Hapsburg Empire*
(91) B. Huldermann, *Albert Ballin* (Cassell, 1922)
(92) Schmitt, *Coming of the War*, Volume I
(93) Pierre Renouvin, *The Immediate Origins of the War* (New Haven, 1928)
(94) Albertini, Volume III
(95) Asquith, *Genesis of The War*
(96) *British Documents on the Origins of the War, 1898–1914*, Volume III
(97) Churchill, *World Crisis*, Memo to Grey, 23rd August, 1912
(98) Bethmann, *Reflections*
(99) Moltke, *Reminiscences*
(100) *Ibid*
(101) Asquith, *Genesis of The War*
(102) Churchill, *World Crisis*
(103) *The Times*, 28th July, 1914
(104) Churchill, *World Crisis*
(105) *Ibid*
(106) Albertini, Volume III
(107) William II, *Memoirs 1878–1918* (November, 1922)
(108) Asquith, *Genesis of The War*
(109) Speech by Grey (3rd August, 1914)
(110) *The Times* (3rd August, 1914)
(111) Churchill, *World Crisis*
(112) *The Times* (5th August 1914)

FURTHER READING

Albertini, Luigi, *The Origins of the War of 1914*, 3 vols; translated and edited by Isabella M. Massey (Oxford University Press, 1965)

Asquith, Henry Herbert, *The Genesis of the War* (New York and London, 1923)

Barnett, C., *The Swordbearers* (London, 1963)

Churchill, W. S., *The World Crisis*, 6 vols (London, 1923–31)

Craig, G. A., *The Politics of the Prussian Army* (Oxford, 1964)

Demeter, K., *The German Officer Corps* (London, 1965)

Earle, E. M., *The Makers of Modern Strategy* (Princeton, 1961)

Fay, Sidney B., *The Origins of the World War* (New York, 1930)

Fleming, D.F., *The Origins and Legacies of World War One* (London, 1968)

Görlitz, W., *The German General Staff* (New York, 1953)

Howard, M. E., *The Franco-Prussian War* (London, 1967)

Ritter, G., *The Schlieffen Plan* (New York, 1958)

Seton-Watson, R.W., *Sarajevo* (London, 1926)

Zeman, *The Break-up of the Hapsburg Empire* (Oxford, 1951)

APPENDIX 1: TIMETABLE TO WAR

1870	July 19	Franco–Prussian war opens
	September 2	French surrender at Sedan
	October 27	French surrender at Metz
1871	May 10	Treaty of Frankfurt
1878	July 13	Treaty of Berlin
1879	October 1	Austro–German alliance
1881	June 18	Three Emperors' League
1882	May 20	Triple Alliance
1887	June 18	Reinsurance Treaty
1890	March	Bismarck resigns
1894	January 4	Franco–Russian alliance
1899	October 11	Boer war opens
1900	June 12	German Navy Law
1902	January 30	Anglo–Japanese agreement
	May 31	Boer war ends
1904	February 8	Russo–Japanese war begins
	April 8	Anglo–French agreement
1905		Schlieffen Plan finalised
	March 22	German Emperor visits Tangier
	September 5	Russo–Japanese war ends with Treaty of Portsmouth
1906	January 16	Algeciras Conference opens
	April 17	Algeciras Conference ends
1907	August 31	Anglo–Russian agreement
1908	October 5	Bulgaria becomes independent

October 6	Austria–Hungary declares annexation of Bosnia–Herzegovina
1909 October 24	Italian–Russian agreement on Balkans
1911 July 1	Panther arrives at Agadir
July 21	Lloyd George Mansion House speech warning Germany
1912 October 8	First Balkan war opens
1913 May 30	First Balkan war ends with Treaty of London
June 29	Second Balkan war begins
August 10	Second Balkan war ends with Treaty of Bucharest
1914 June 28	Ferdinand assassinated at Sarajevo
July 23	Austrian ultimatum sent to Serbia
July 25	Serbian reply rejected
July 26	Austrian mobilisation against Serbia
July 28	Austrian declaration of war; hostilities begin
July 29	Russia orders partial mobilisation
July 31	Austrian and Russian full mobilisations German ultimatum to Russia
August 1	Germany orders general mobilisation Germany declares war on Russia France orders mobilisation
August 2	German ultimatum to Belgium German troops move into Luxemburg
August 4	British ultimatum to Germany Britain declares war against Germany Germany declares war against Belgium

APPENDIX 2: DRAMATIS PERSONAE

AEHRENTHAL, Alois, Baron Lex (Count after 1909), Austro–Hungarian Ambassador at St Petersburg 1899–1906, Minister for Foreign Affairs 1906–12

ALEXANDER II, Tzar of Russia 1855, assassinated 1881

ALEXANDER III, Tzar of Russia 1881–94

ASQUITH, Herbert Henry, British Prime Minister 1908–16

AUFFENBERG, General von Ritter, Austro–Hungarian War Minister 1911–12

BALFOUR, British Prime Minister 1902–5, Foreign Secretary 1916–19, 1st Earl of Balfour 1922

BEACONSFIELD, Earl of (Benjamin Disraeli), British Prime Minister until defeated by Gladstone in 1880, died 1881

BECK, Count von, Austrian Prime Minister 1906–8

BECK, Count von, General, Austro–Hungarian Chief of Staff 1881–1906

BENCKENDORFF, Count Alexander, Russian Ambassador to London 1903–17

BERCHTOLD, Count von Leopold, Austrian Ambassador to St Petersburg, 1906–11, Foreign Minister 1912–15

BERTIE, Sir F., British Ambassador to Paris 1905–18

BETHMANN HOLLWEG, von T., German Minister for the Interior 1907–9, Chancellor 1909–17

BISMARCK, Herbert, Secretary of State to the German Foreign Ministry 1886–90

BISMARCK, Prince Otto, German Chancellor 1871–90

BOGIČEVIĆ, Miloš, Serbian Chargé d'Affaires at Berlin 1906–14

BOULANGER, General, French War Minister 1886–7

BOURGEOIS, Léon, French Prime Minister 1896, Foreign Minister 1906

BRATIANU, Joan, Roumanian Prime Minister and War Minister 1914–18

BRIAND, Aristide, French Prime Minister 1909–11

BÜLOW, Prince Bernard, German Ambassador to Rome 1893–7, Foreign Secretary 1897–1900, Chancellor 1900–9

CAMBON, Jules, French Ambassador to Berlin 1907–14

CAMBON, Paul, French Ambassador to London 1898–1920

CAMPBELL-BANNERMAN, Sir Henry, British Prime Minister 1905–8

CAPRIVI, General Leon von, German Chancellor 1890–4

CAROL I, Roumanian King 1881–1914

CARTWRIGHT, Sir Fairfax, British Ambassador to Vienna 1908–13

CHAMBERLAIN, Joseph, British Colonial Secretary 1895–1903

CHURCHILL, Winston, British Under-Secretary of State for Colonies 1906–8, President of the Board of Trade 1908–10, Home Secretary 1910–11, First Lord of the Admiralty 1911–15

CLEMENCEAU, Georges, French Prime Minister 1906–9

CONRAD, von Hotzendorf, Chief of the Austrian General Staff 1906–11

CORTI, Count Luigi, Italian Minister for Foreign Affairs, Ambassador to London 1885–8

CRISPI, Francesco, Italian Minister for Home Affairs 1877, Foreign Minister 1887, Prime Minister 1887–91

DELCASSÉ, Théophile, Foreign Minister, 1898–1905, French Minister of Marine 1911–13, Ambassador to St Petersburg 1913–14

DERBY, Earl of, British Foreign Minister 1874–8

DOUMERGUE, Gaston, French Prime Minister and Foreign Minister 1913–14

EDWARD VII, King of England, 1901–10

EULENBURG, Prince Philip, German Ambassador to Vienna 1894–1901, 1902–7

FALLIÈRES, Armand, President of France 1906–13

FRANCIS FERDINAND, Austro–Hungarian Archduke and Heir Apparent, assassinated at Sarajevo 1914

FRANCIS JOSEPH, Emperor of Austria and King of Hungary 1848–1916

GEORGE V, King of England 1910–36

GIOLITTI, Giovanni, Italian Prime Minister 1906–9, 1911–14

GLADSTONE, William Ewart, British Prime Minister 1868–74, 1881–4, 1886–92, 1894

GOLUCHOWSKI, Count Agenor, Austrian Foreign Minister 1895–1906

GRANVILLE, George Leveson-Gower, British Foreign Minister 1870–4, 1880–5

GREY, Sir Edward (Viscount Grey of Fallodon after 1916), British Foreign Secretary 1905–16

HALDANE, R. B. (Viscount after 1911), British Secretary of State for War 1905–12

HARDINGE, Sir Charles (Baron after 1910), British Assistant Under Secretary, Foreign Affairs 1903–4, Ambassador to St Petersburg 1904–6, Permanent Under Secretary, Foreign Affairs 1906–10

HOLSTEIN, Baron Friedrich von, German Foreign Office 1880–1906

IZVOLSKY, Alexander, Russian Foreign Minister 1906–10, Ambassador to Paris 1910–17

JAGOW, Gottlieb von, German Ambassador to Rome, 1909–12, Secretary of State at Foreign Ministry 1913–16

JOFFRE, Joseph, Chief of French General Staff 1911–14

KALNOKY, Count, Austrian Foreign Minister 1881–95

KIDERLEN-WÄCHTER, Alfred von, German Minister at Bucharest 1899–1910, Foreign Minister 1910–12

LAMSDORF, Count, Russian Foreign Minister 1901–6

LANSDOWNE, Marquess, British Foreign Secretary 1900–5

LICHNOWSKY, Prince von, First Secretary, German Embassy at Vienna 1896, Ambassador to London 1912–14

LLOYD GEORGE, David, British Chancellor of the Exchequer 1908–15, Prime Minister 1916–22

MCKENNA, R., First Lord of the Admiralty until 1911

MARSCHALL, von Bieberstein, Baron, German Secretary of State for Foreign Affairs 1890–7, Ambassador at Constantinople 1897–1912, Ambassador to London 1912

METTERNICH, Count Paul von Wolff, German Ambassador to London 1901–12

MOLTKE, Hellmuth von (the Elder), Prussian Chief of the General Staff 1868–90

MOLTKE, Hellmuth von (the Younger), Prussian–German Chief of the General Staff 1906–14

NICHOLAS II, Tzar 1894–1917

NICOLSON, Sir Arthur (Baron Carnock after 1916), British Ambassador to Madrid 1905–6, to St Petersburg 1906–10, Permanent Under-Secretary of State, Foreign Affairs 1910–16

PAŠIĆ, Nicholas, Serbian Prime Minister 1906–18

POINCARÉ, Raymond, French Finance Minister 1906, Prime Minister and Foreign Minister 1912–13, President 1913–20

POLLIO, General, Italian Chief of Staff 1908–14

RODD, Sir J. Rennell, British Ambassador to Rome 1908–21

ROUVIER, Maurice, French Prime Minister 1905–6

SALISBURY, Robert Cecil, Marquess, British Secretary of State, Foreign Affairs 1878–80, 1885–6, 1887–92, 1895–1900, Prime Minister 1895–1902

SAN GIULIANO, Antonio, Marches di, Italian Foreign Minister, 1905–6, 1910–14, Ambassador to London 1906–10

SAZONOV, Serge, Russian Embassy Counsellor, London 1904–6, Acting Foreign Minister 1909–10, Foreign Minister 1910–16

SCHOEN, Freiherr Wilhelm, German Ambassador at St Petersburg 1907, Secretary of State, Foreign Affairs 1907–10, Ambassador to Paris 1910–14

SCHLIEFFEN, General von, German Chief of Staff 1891–1906

SZÖGYENY-MARICH, Count, Austrian Ambassador to Berlin 1892–1914

TISZA, Count Stephen, Hungarian Prime Minister 1904, 1913–14

TITTONI, Tommaso, Italian Foreign Minister 1903–5, 1906–9, Ambassador to Paris 1910–17

VIVIANI, Réne, French Prime Minister 1914–15

WILHELM I, German Emperor 1861–88

WILHELM II, German Emperor 1888–1918

WILSON, General Sir Henry, British Chief of Staff 1913

ZIMMERMANN, Alfred, German Under-Secretary of State, Foreign Affairs 1911–16

PICTURE CREDITS

The Publishers wish to thank the following for permission to reproduce the illustrations on the pages mentioned: Trustees of the National Maritime Museum, 87; the L.E.A., 22, 24, 25, 35, 40, 56, 59, 68, 87, 88, 92, 102; the Weaver-Smith Collection, frontispiece, 14, 32, 36, 39, 45, 48, 51, 53, 90; the Mansell Collection, jacket, 11, 16, 23, 29, 30, 50, 78, 96, 107, 108, 114; the Radio Times Hulton Picture Library, 96 (centre); Paul Popper, 12; John Freeman & Co., 64. Other illustrations appearing in this book are the property of the Wayland Picture Library.

ACKNOWLEDGEMENT

The following documentary extracts are Crown Copyright and are reproduced by permission of the Controller of Her Majesty's Stationery Office: details of the Austro–German Alliance, 1879 (p. 39); Foreign Office Statement, 1915, on the rejection of the German alliance formula, 1912 (p. 65); the memorandum by Sir Edward Grey, 1906, (p. 104).

INDEX